CW00553159

WILDLIFE

Marine Mammals, Seabirds, Fish,
and Other Sea Life

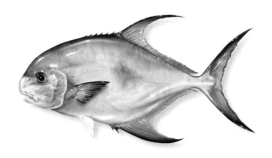

A Field Guide to

NORTH ATLANTIC
WILDLIFE

Marine Mammals, Seabirds, Fish,
and Other Sea Life

NOBLE S. PROCTOR

PATRICK J. LYNCH

Illustrated by
PATRICK J. LYNCH

Yale University Press
New Haven and London

Designed by Patrick J. Lynch.
Set in Adobe Utopia and Adobe Univers typefaces.
Printed in Italy by EuroGrafica SpA.

ISBN 0-300-10658-0
Library of Congress Control Number: 2004117308

The paper in this book meets the guidelines for permanence and durability of
the Committee on Production Guidelines for Book Longevity of the Council on
Library Resources.

10 9 8 7 6 5 4 3 2 1

To Carolyn, Adam, and Eric

To Susan and Devorah

CONTENTS

PREFACE

This book has been several years in the making, but in a sense we've been preparing it for thirty years and more – on countless pelagic trips on most of the world's oceans and on every type of trip to the North Atlantic, from day-fishing boats to four-day runs out to the continental shelf. We couldn't possibly list the captains and crews of all these boats here, but we thank them all for the opportunity to view and enjoy the offshore environment and animals of the North Atlantic.

We also thank the fishing parties of day boats, dock fishermen, and crew members of fishing boats for patiently allowing us to look at, poke and prod, document, and discuss the many interesting fish they brought ashore or caught and released. And we are very grateful to the hundreds of fellow birders and whale watchers we have shared a deck with, and for the privilege of sharing their knowledge, enthusiasm, and deep concern for the fate of our fragile offshore environment.

Many individuals have spent time sharing their data, knowledge of specific species, and continued support of this project. We especially thank the crew and staff of the Dolphin Fleet for many trips to the exciting waters off Cape Cod. During various pelagic trips Davis Finch, Frank Gallo, Frank Gardiner, Dr. Roger Payne, Diana Payne, Dr. Charles "Stormy" Mayo, Fred Sibley, Don Sinotti, Dr. Jeffrey Spendelow, James Stone, and Dr. Frank Trainor have shared their time and expertise with us.

Those who have lent their support, expertise, and comments as the book took shape include Dawn Alicandro, Margaret Ardwin, David Bolinsky, Cheryl Burack, Daniel Cinotti, Frank Gallo, Patty Harris, Sarah Horton, Sean Jackson, Carl Jaffe, Toini Jaffe, Janet Jeddrey, Jane Lederer, Rick Leone, Devorah Lynch, Howard Newstadt, Kimberly Pasko, Wayne Petersen, Roger Tory Peterson, Fred Richards, Sally Richards, Stacy Ruwe, Fred Sibley, Phillip Simon, Virginia Simon, Dr. Jeffrey Spendelow, and Alex and Tyler Wack. We greatly appreciate everything these friends have contributed to this field guide.

We extend a special thank you to Jean Thomson Black, senior editor for life sciences at Yale University Press, for her faith in us over the years and for being our champion at the Press to see that this book came to fruition.

We also thank manuscript editor Laura Jones Dooley for her thorough dedication to editorial quality and for always making us seem much more articulate than we really are.

And of course, our special thanks go to our wives and families:

For Noble – to Carolyn, Adam, and Eric, who I am sure had wished I was home or available at times of long offshore trips or during periods of writing.

For Pat – to dearest Zhu, and to Devorah, Alex, and Tyler, who make it all worthwhile.

Without their support and love, any accomplishments would be empty.

NOBLE S. PROCTOR
Branford, Connecticut

PATRICK J. LYNCH
North Haven, Connecticut
www.patricklynch.net

INTRODUCTION

This guide is designed to be a useful companion for the thousands of people who every year boat, fish, watch whales, look for seabirds, and otherwise enjoy the magnificent offshore environment of the northwestern North Atlantic Ocean along North America's eastern shore. The "save the whales" environmental movement of the 1970s sharply increased awareness of and public interest in marine mammal and seabird populations off the eastern seaboard. And the collapse in the past thirty years of the North Atlantic fishing industry is a strong reminder of how fragile the huge ocean really is and how quickly we are losing marine resources to overfishing, pollution, and the destruction of coastal habitats, which feed our offshore waters and provide crucial breeding grounds for many marine species.

The losses in offshore areas like the Grand Banks of Newfoundland can hardly be exaggerated. Nineteenth-century fishermen spoke of cod so plentiful that you could "walk across the sea on their backs." Now fisheries for every significant commercial fish species on the Grand Banks have collapsed or are sharply restricted. In 1995, Canada's government suspended the once-bountiful cod and flounder fisheries. We hope that this guide can make a small contribution to increasing public awareness of the offshore environment in addition to providing enjoyment to the growing number of people who enjoy seabirds, marine mammals, sportfishing, and the natural history and beauty of our offshore environment.

Fishing for cod on the Grand Banks, 1930s. Photo: National Archives of Canada

INTRODUCTION

The Northwestern North Atlantic

This field guide covers the major marine life of the northwestern North Atlantic from Labrador and Newfoundland in the north to Cape Hatteras in the south (see the regional map on the following pages). The offshore environments in this region of the Atlantic Ocean range from the subpolar seas off Canada's Maritime Provinces to the subtropical Gulf Stream currents just off the North Carolina coast.

The Gulf Stream and Gulf Stream gyres. Adapted from NOAA satellite images

Two major oceanographic features dominate the marine habitats of the eastern seaboard: the collision and mixing of two ocean currents, and the large shallow areas, or "banks," that lie along the continental shelf from Cape Cod north to Newfoundland. The cold Labrador current descends southward from the Arctic Ocean along the Labrador and Newfoundland coasts, and the warm Gulf Stream current flows northward from Florida along the southeastern coast of the United States before curving northeast off Cape Hatteras toward the mid-Atlantic Ocean and northern Europe. The convergence of these two contrasting streams of cold and warm water causes the characteristic foggy offshore weather over the Grand Banks and south to Nova Scotia,the Gulf of Maine, and New England. The Labrador current also brings nutrient-laden and oxygen-rich waters over the massive Grand Banks and to the smaller banks scattered along the Canadian Maritimes and New England coasts. Even though the fish populations of the Grand Banks are now severely depleted by overfishing, these shallow waters once combined with the warmth of the Gulf Stream and the rich nutrients from the Labrador current to create one of the most biologically rich and productive environments on earth. And even though the Gulf Stream curves well offshore north of Cape Hatteras, its warming influence often brings tropical and subtropical fish, marine mammals, and seabirds into the New York Bight, the Georges Bank off Cape Cod, and the waters off Nova Scotia.

Most of the species described in this field guide inhabit the relatively shallow waters of the continental shelf or inshore coastal areas. Water depth, however, has a great influence on marine habitats and animal populations, and the edge of the continental shelf is best thought of as a separate environment with a set of inhabitants seldom seen in shallower waters. For example, Sperm Whales, Sei Whales, and Grampus (Risso's Dolphin) are more common in deep waters well offshore and much less common in the shallow waters of the continental shelf. Water depth also explains why areas like the Hudson Canyon are so attractive to birders, whale watchers, and sportfishers. The canyon's deep waters are hundreds of miles closer to shore than

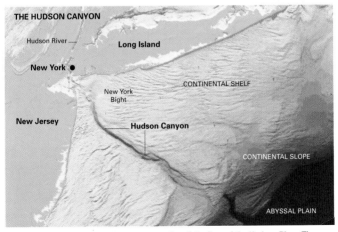

The Hudson Canyon is an underwater extension of the flow of the Hudson River. The canyon's deeper waters bring deep-ocean animals closer to the coastline to the benefit of birders, whale watchers, and sportfishers. Photo: adapted from USGS imaging, based on NOAA bathymetry data

THE NORTHWESTERN NORTH ATLANTIC

QUEBEC

GASPÉ PENINSULA

QUEBEC

ST. LAWRENCE RIVER

Québec

NEW BRUNSWICK

MAINE

BAY OF FUNDY

NOVA SCOTIA

La Have B

Jeffreys Bank

NEW HAMPSHIRE

GULF OF MAINE

Browns Bank

Jeffreys Ledge

MASSACHUSETTS

Boston

Stellwagen Bank

Providence

−12 m

Georges Bank

NEW YORK

MV

NI

Coxes Ledge

Nantucket Shoals

Great South Channel

New York

Lydonia Canyon

NEW JERSEY

NEW YORK BIGHT

"The Canyons" area

Oceanographer Canyon

Philadelphia

Ambrose Light

Hydrographer Canyon

Hudson Canyon

Washington DC

Atlantic City

CAPE MAY

−4218 m

DELAWARE BAY

Baltimore Canyon

Hudson Canyon

CHESAPEAKE BAY

VIRGINIA

Washington Canyon

Norfolk Canyon

Norfolk

−26 m

ALBEMARLE SOUND

CAPE HATTERAS

NORTH CAROLINA

"The Point"

−5118 m

Hatteras Canyon

Diamond Shoals

PAMLICO SOUND

HATTERAS PLAIN

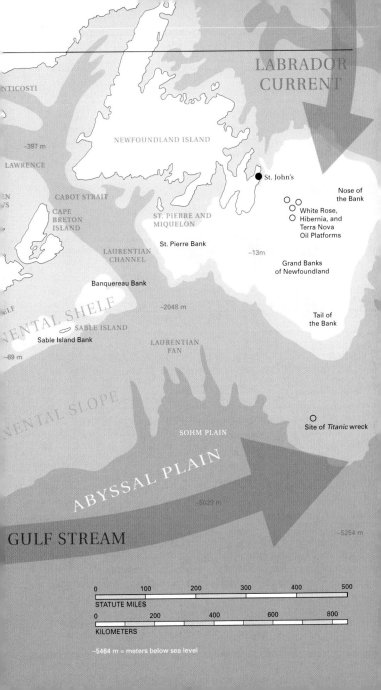

LABRADOR
CURRENT

ANTICOSTI

NEWFOUNDLAND ISLAND

−397 m

LAWRENCE

EN
WS

CABOT STRAIT

● St. John's

CAPE
BRETON
ISLAND

ST. PIERRE AND
MIQUELON

○ ○
○ ○   White Rose,
○   Hibernia, and
         Terra Nova
         Oil Platforms

Nose of
the Bank

LAURENTIAN
CHANNEL

St. Pierre Bank

−13m

Grand Banks
of Newfoundland

Banquereau Bank

−2048 m

Tail of
the Bank

ELF

NENTAL SHELF

SABLE ISLAND

LAURENTIAN
FAN

Sable Island Bank

−69 m

NENTAL SLOPE

SOHM PLAIN

○ Site of *Titanic* wreck

ABYSSAL PLAIN

−5029 m

GULF STREAM

−5254 m

0	100	200	300	400	500

STATUTE MILES

0	200	400	600	800

KILOMETERS

−5464 m = meters below sea level

is the true edge of the continental shelf, and many deep-water species move into the canyon to feed.

Conservation

Today's marine environment faces a myriad of problems, many of which we can have a direct influence on improving. Pollution, overfishing, the use of nets that are lethal to species other than targeted food fish, oil spills, and the continued killing of whales for "scientific" studies have had a devastating impact on many marine species.

At one time the Atlantic Cod was the foundation of the east coast fishing industry. Cod were viewed much as the Passenger Pigeon was, occurring in numbers so vast that any type of harvesting would scarcely affect their numbers. The supply of cod, it seemed, would never run out. Today, however, cod are so low in numbers and individual cod are so small that many offshore areas can no longer be fished. Billfish (swordfish, marlins) have also plunged in numbers and in average size of individuals. Formerly obscure species such as the Patagonian Tooth Fish (renamed the Chilean Sea Bass to make the species more marketable) have seen a dramatic reduction in numbers after just a few years as a sought-after food fish. The long-line technique of fishing for sea bass and other popular species of food fish has had a negative impact on seabirds, which dive for the baited lines and are drowned once hooked. Thousands of albatross, cormorants, and boobies die each year as accidental victims of long-line fishing.

While walking beaches in various parts of the world we are continually appalled by the amount of litter and fishing trash cast up by the tides. We have walked Alaskan beaches where debris from monofilament fishing nets, and the remains of dead sea life entangled in them, line the coast for miles. These accidental victims range from fish to seabirds, seals, and marine otters. Old monofilament causes yet more damage when seabirds unknowingly use it as nesting material; monofilament line often entangles and traps chicks in the nest, dooming the young birds to starvation or strangulation.

Since the 1970s, the plight of our large whale species has become a popular environmental cause that has helped direct attention to the ongoing devastation of our ocean environment. Through active participation of conservation groups, and the combined voices of many concerned people, most of our larger whale species have received protection from immediate extinction. In the United States, the Marine Mammal Protection Act of 1972 was a giant step forward to protect these amazing animals. But we must remain vigilant. Today some whale species are still harvested. Only the continued attention of a concerned public, plus genuine scientific research into the biology and natural history of these remarkable animals, will ensure that our children and grandchildren will be able to see for themselves the largest animals ever to have lived on earth. Stay informed, eat seafood responsibly, speak out, and support genuine marine biological research. If you enjoy the offshore environment, *then act to protect it*. Today *we* are the stewards of our environment, and if we lose these precious ocean resources through our ignorance, greed, or indifference, we will have caused an immeasurable loss to future generations of humanity.

Red List Species
The common names of endangered or threatened marine species listed in this guide are printed in red. For more information on each species, see the IUCN Red List of Endangered Species Web site, at:

http://www.redlist.org/

About the species range maps
The maps in this field guide are general approximations of the seasonal ranges of each species. In many marine species the exact extent of their seasonal and geographic ranges is not well documented, and fish, whales, and seabirds are highly mobile creatures that move freely throughout the Northwestern Atlantic following winds and weather, ocean currents, and seasonal movements of their prey species.

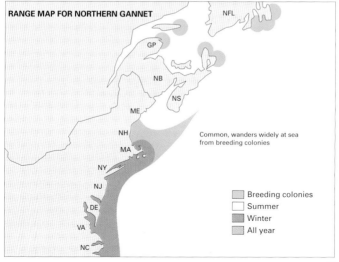

RANGE MAP FOR NORTHERN GANNET

Common, wanders widely at sea from breeding colonies

Breeding colonies
Summer
Winter
All year

TOPOGRAPHY OF SHARKS AND RAYS

A quick overview of common topographic terminology, particularly of structures typically referred to in field descriptions

TYPICAL SHARK

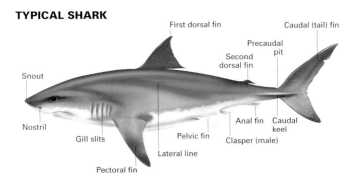

First dorsal fin

Caudal (tail) fin

Precaudal pit

Second dorsal fin

Snout

Nostril

Gill slits

Pelvic fin

Anal fin

Caudal keel

Clasper (male)

Lateral line

Pectoral fin

DOGFISH

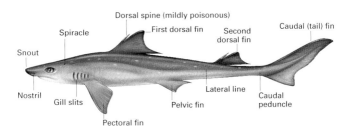

Dorsal spine (mildly poisonous)

First dorsal fin

Second dorsal fin

Caudal (tail) fin

Spiracle

Snout

Nostril

Gill slits

Lateral line

Caudal peduncle

Pelvic fin

Pectoral fin

RAY

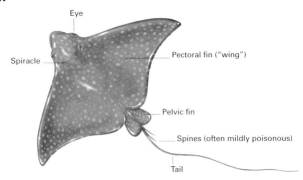

Eye

Spiracle

Pectoral fin ("wing")

Pelvic fin

Spines (often mildly poisonous)

Tail

SPINY-RAYED FISH

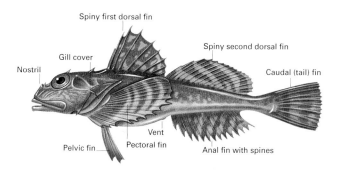

Spiny first dorsal fin
Spiny second dorsal fin
Caudal (tail) fin
Gill cover
Nostril
Vent
Pelvic fin
Pectoral fin
Anal fin with spines

TYPICAL FISH

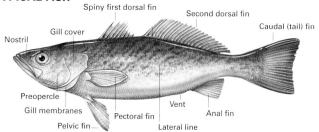

Spiny first dorsal fin
Second dorsal fin
Caudal (tail) fin
Gill cover
Nostril
Preopercle
Gill membranes
Pectoral fin
Vent
Anal fin
Pelvic fin
Lateral line

TUNA

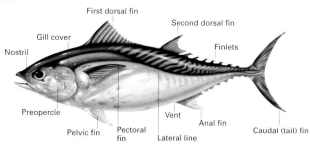

First dorsal fin
Second dorsal fin
Finlets
Gill cover
Nostril
Preopercle
Pelvic fin
Pectoral fin
Vent
Anal fin
Lateral line
Caudal (tail) fin

TOPOGRAPHY OF BIRDS

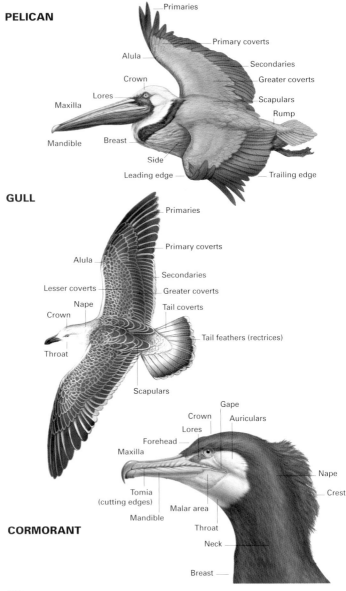

PELICAN

Primaries

Primary coverts

Alula

Secondaries

Crown

Greater coverts

Lores

Scapulars

Maxilla

Rump

Mandible

Breast

Side

Leading edge

Trailing edge

GULL

Primaries

Primary coverts

Alula

Secondaries

Lesser coverts

Greater coverts

Nape

Tail coverts

Crown

Throat

Tail feathers (rectrices)

Scapulars

Gape

Crown

Auriculars

Lores

Forehead

Maxilla

Nape

Crest

Tomia
(cutting edges)

Malar area

Mandible

Throat

Neck

Breast

CORMORANT

TOPOGRAPHY OF TURTLES, WHALES, AND DOLPHINS

SEA TURTLE

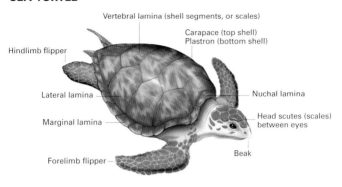

Vertebral lamina (shell segments, or scales)

Carapace (top shell)
Plastron (bottom shell)

Hindlimb flipper

Lateral lamina

Nuchal lamina

Marginal lamina

Head scutes (scales) between eyes

Forelimb flipper

Beak

TYPICAL DOLPHIN

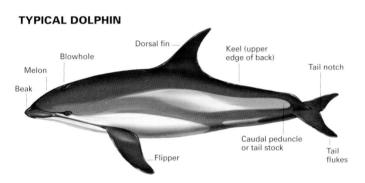

Dorsal fin

Keel (upper edge of back)

Blowhole

Tail notch

Melon

Beak

Caudal peduncle or tail stock

Flipper

Tail flukes

HUMPBACK WHALE

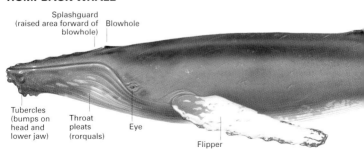

Splashguard (raised area forward of blowhole)

Blowhole

Tubercles (bumps on head and lower jaw)

Throat pleats (rorquals)

Eye

Flipper

A Field Guide to
NORTH ATLANTIC WILDLIFE

Marine Mammals, Seabirds, Fish,
and Other Sea Life

PLATES

PELAGIC ALGAE

Seaweeds, or marine algae, are associated mainly with inshore rocks, shallow bottoms, and fringes of offshore islands. Most are firmly anchored to a substrate and thus are not part of the true marine community. Marine algae known as Rockweed cover breakwaters and jetties, where they are easy to see, especially at low tide. Well offshore two other species of marine algae are regularly seen. Knotted Wrack grows attached to rocks alongshore but because of its inflated bladders often drifts offshore in great masses, forming large mats. Phalaropes and other birds feed on the invertebrate life associated with these algae. The only true marine (pelagic) group of seaweeds are the Gulfweeds (*Sargassum* spp.). These free-floating mats, as the name implies, are seen most often in the warm waters of the Gulf Stream. The algal clumps are host to a complex community of invertebrates and fish, such as the amazingly camouflaged Sargassumfish. Because of the abundance of life associated with marine algae, birds and fish find these dense mats very attractive as feeding areas. Mats of Gulfweed can grow to vast size in the waters off Bermuda, in the becalmed region known as the Sargasso Sea.

ROCKWEED   *Fucus* spp.

A common brown seaweed growing on rocks and jetties along coasts. Most people are familiar with Rockweed's swollen, bumpy branch tips, which pop when you squeeze or step on them. Two bladders side by side on stipe. Mats of these algae occasionally drift far offshore.

KNOTTED WRACK   *Ascophyllum nodosum*

A common brown algae of bays and rocky shores. Note single and numerous large bladders on stipe. Because of its buoyancy, often found in large mats well offshore.

GULFWEED   *Sargassum natans* and *S. fluitans*

True pelagic ocean drifters. Note small bladders on branching tips and leaf-like flattened blades. Separation of species based on appearance of bladders. *S. natans* has small spikes at bladder tip; *S. fluitans* lacks this feature. Gulfweeds prefer warm waters but drift northward in large mats in Gulf Stream.

ROCKWEED

Paired air
bladders on
stipe

KNOTTED WRACK

SARGASSUMFISH
Histrio histrio

Air
bladders
within
stipe

GULFWEED
Sargassum fluitans

S. fluitans
has simple
berry-like
bladders

Sargassum natans
S. natans has bladders
tipped with a small
spike

3

JELLYFISH

Siphonophores and jellyfish are two groups that are often confused and lumped as one group. They are distinctly different animals, however. **Siphonophores** are hydrozoans, which have an attached tree-like (hydra) stage and a free-floating (medusa) stage. Siphonophores exhibit an extreme form of this combination: they are complex colonies of medusae and polyps. The Portuguese Man-Of-War is an excellent example. Siphonophores also have a velum (sail) because they are planktonic (weak swimmers) and drift with the wind. **Jellyfish (Scyphozoa)** are large marine medusae whose polyp stage is either lacking or reduced to an extremely small form. True jellyfish are free-swimming and lack a velum.

BY-THE-WIND SAILOR   *Velella velella*

Small platform structure with brownish, flattened central sail (velum). Below disk, mass of tentacle-like structures up to 5 in. (12.5 cm) long, with feeding and reproductive flaps. A true marine form. Rapidly disintegrates once it drifts inshore and water salinity drops. **Range:** Tropical waters worldwide. **Float size:** To 4 in. (10 cm).

PORTUGUESE MAN-OF-WAR   *Physalia physalia*

Well known for its painful stings. Powder blue, balloon-like transparent float visible at the water's surface. Elongate tentacle-like processes and curtain-like folds hang below inflated float and may extend more than 50 ft. (15 m). Beware of tentacles, which can sting long after animal's death. **Float size:** To 1 ft. (30 cm).

SEA NETTLE   *Chrysaora quinquecirrha*

A large jellyfish with a smooth to slightly pebbly bell surface. Tentacles emerge from distinct clefts on bell edge. Two distinct forms. Marine form is larger (to 7 in., 18 cm), with more tentacles (up to 40) and with pink lines on bell. Estuarine and bay form is smaller (to 4 in., 10 cm), with 24 tentacles. Sting is very painful. **Range:** Cape Cod south to West Indies. Very common in Chesapeake Bay and other tidal areas. Water salinity determines range limits.

SEA WASP   *Tamoya haplonema*

Rigid bell with four distinct tentacles, each with flattened, paddle-like base and elongated filament. A strong and fast swimmer, tending to stay near sea bottom. Sting is extremely painful; use caution. **Range:** Mainly tropical; on occasion drifts north as far as Long Island. **Float size:** To 4 in. (10 cm).

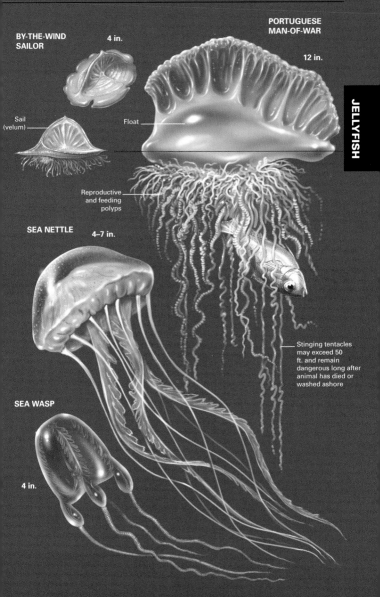

JELLYFISH

BY-THE-WIND SAILOR

4 in.

Sail (velum)

PORTUGUESE MAN-OF-WAR

12 in.

Float

Reproductive and feeding polyps

SEA NETTLE

4–7 in.

Stinging tentacles may exceed 50 ft. and remain dangerous long after animal has died or washed ashore

SEA WASP

4 in.

5

MOON JELLY   *Aurelia aurita*

Familiar jellyfish of bays, sounds, and inland waters. Bell edge rimmed by short fringe of tentacles. Prey captured in mucilaginous cap and "cleared off" for ingestion by elongate mouth arms that drape below. Easily identified by distinct shamrock appearance of gonads seen through transparent cap. **Range:** Extreme northern Greenland to Caribbean. **Size:** To 10 in. (25 cm).

LION'S MANE   *Cyanea capillata*

The world's largest jellyfish. Typically to 12 in. (30 cm) but can reach 8 ft. (2.4 m). Most specimens south of Cape Hatteras are small (to 5 in., 12.5 cm), but individuals increase in size in North Atlantic. A classic jellyfish, ranging in color from brownish to pink. Extremely long tentacles and massive cascading group of mouth lobes. **Range:** North Atlantic to Carolinas.

MUSHROOM CAP   *Rhopilema verrilli*

No tentacles below thick, high-domed bell. Cream colored with brownish yellow marks on mouth lobes. Mainly marine, but can be blown into sounds and bays under certain wind conditions. **Range:** Uncommon off Carolinas and south. A rare stray north of Cape Hatteras. **Size:** To 12 in. (30 cm).

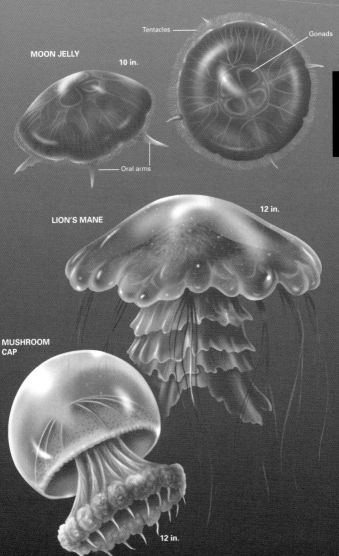

MOON JELLY

10 in.

Tentacles

Gonads

Oral arms

LION'S MANE

12 in.

MUSHROOM CAP

12 in.

CTENOPHORES (COMB JELLIES)

Often mistaken for jellyfish. However, comb jellies do not sting, have two tentacles or lobes below their sac-like body, and have up to eight comb-like ciliary plates. Gelatinous and fragile, they turn into nondescript blobs out of water. All are plankters (drifters with little self-locomotion) and can amass in large swarms. They are predators of small fish and fish eggs. *Note:* when viewing comb jellies, look for pinkish worm-like forms in the gut region. These are the parasitic young of the Burrowing Anemone (*Edwardsia leidyi*).

SEA GOOSEBERRY   *Pleurobrachia pileus*

Walnut-shaped body. Commonly drifts into inshore waters and washes up on beaches, where contractile tentacles cannot be seen. Incredible numbers can be washed into bays. Colorless and hard to see in water. **Size:** To 1.2 in. (28 mm).

NORTHERN COMB JELLY   *Bolinopsis infundibulum*

Lobes shorter than oval body. Most common comb jelly in northern New England coastal waters. Transparent and hard to see in water. Like all comb jellies, can occur in amazingly large numbers. **Size:** To 6 in. (15 cm).

SEA WALNUT   *Mnemiopsis leidyi*

Body more flattened than Northern Comb Jelly. Lobes longer than body sphere. When disturbed, bright green bioluminescent flashes occur all along combs. Most common comb jelly south of Cape Cod. **Size:** To 4 in. (10 cm).

BEROE'S COMB JELLY   *Beroe* spp.

A transparent, somewhat flattened sac. Pinkish to rust colored with comb rows on bell and no tentacles. Two species occur regularly on the east coast: *B. ovata*, Chesapeake Bay and south, and *B. cucumis*, common in northern Gulf of Maine. Separation to species can be difficult, even when specimens are in hand. **Size:** To 4.5 in. (11 cm).

VENUS GIRDLE   *Cestum veneris*

Unmistakable Gulf Stream species. Flattened like a belt with central constriction. Two rows of combs on upper lobe margins. Color greenish to white. Rare drifter out of Gulf Stream to Atlantic waters and inshore. **Size:** To 5 ft. (1.5 m).

CTENOPHORES (COMB JELLIES)

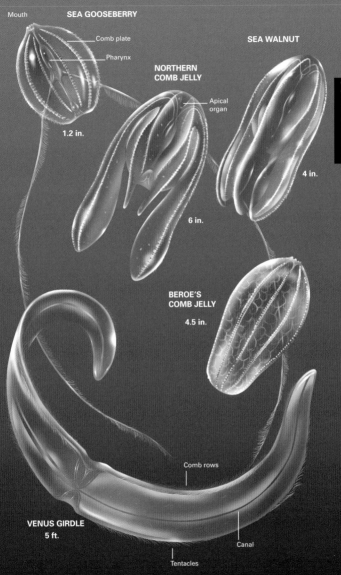

Mouth

SEA GOOSEBERRY

Comb plate

Pharynx

1.2 in.

NORTHERN COMB JELLY

Apical organ

6 in.

SEA WALNUT

4 in.

BEROE'S COMB JELLY

4.5 in.

COMB JELLIES

Comb rows

VENUS GIRDLE
5 ft.

Canal

Tentacles

9

PELAGIC INVERTEBRATES (PLANKTON)

SHELLED SEA BUTTERFLIES
Limacina spp.

Tiny snail-like organisms that sometimes gather in great numbers near the ocean surface. Usually seen at night at surface of deep water well offshore. Shells transparent. Swim by paddling with wing-like parapodia (modified snail feet). **Size:** 0.25 in. (6 mm).

NAKED SEA BUTTERFLY
Clione limacina

Similar in appearance and habits to Shelled Sea Butterflies but larger and lacking hard shell. Paired tentacles on head and three pairs of tentacle-like projections. Swims using wing-like parapodia (modified snail feet). **Size:** 1 in. (25 mm).

ARROW WORMS
Sagitta spp.

Very small predatory worms that swim like tiny fish at the ocean surface, preying on small plankton. Head with hooked claws and tiny eyespots. Two paired fins along length of body, flattened tail. Generally found well offshore. **Size:** 0.75 in. (18 mm).

PLANKTON WORM
Tomopteris helgolandica

Glassy, transparent planktonic worm with centipede-like appearance. Active swimmer, seen at night at surface of offshore waters. Curls into a ball and sinks quickly when touched or frightened. **Size:** To 3.5 in. (89 mm).

OIKOPLEURA
Oikopleura spp.

These tiny invertebrates create gelatinous bubble-like "glass houses" about 0.75 in. (19 mm) in diameter. Look closely for tiny tadpole-like animal within this glass house. Often very common in coastal waters. **Size** (of animal): 0.5 in. (13 mm).

SALPS
Thalia and *Salpa* spp.

Transparent, jelly-like, planktonic animals, similar in size and shape to gel medicine capsules, with open central core through body. Moves by jetting water through body. Sometimes present in huge numbers, generally well offshore but sometimes in coastal waters. **Size:** Varies with species, from less than 0.25 in. (5 mm) to 8.5 in. (210 mm).

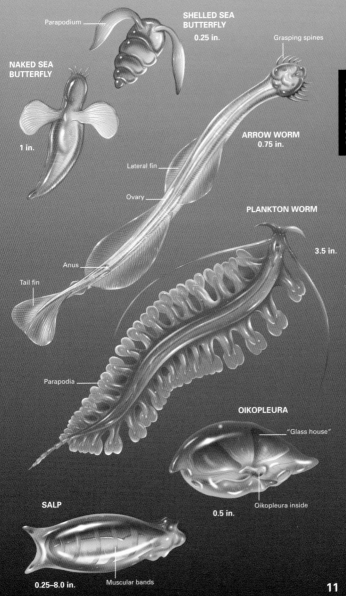

SHELLED SEA BUTTERFLY
0.25 in.

Parapodium

Grasping spines

NAKED SEA BUTTERFLY

1 in.

ARROW WORM
0.75 in.

Lateral fin

Ovary

PLANKTON WORM

3.5 in.

Anus

Tail fin

Parapodia

OIKOPLEURA

"Glass house"

Oikopleura inside

0.5 in.

SALP

0.25–8.0 in.

Muscular bands

CEPHALOPODS

SQUID AND RELATIVES   This is an active and intelligent group of animals. Note the very complex eyes, which rival those of mammals. The head and body of a squid is termed the mantle. Fin shape is very important in the identification of the more common squids encountered in the North Atlantic.

NORTHERN SHORTFIN SQUID   *Illex illecebrosus*

Short triangular fins one-third the length of mantle. In hand, note notch toward front of eye cover. **Range:** Arctic waters to Cape Cod. Notable inshore movement during summer. **Size:** Mantle to 9 in. (23 cm).

LONGFIN INSHORE SQUID   *Loligo pealii*

Fins very long to half the length of mantle and angled. No eye notch. Eaten by wide variety of fish. Most common squid between Cape Cod and Cape Hatteras. **Range:** Bay of Fundy south to Caribbean. **Size:** Mantle to 17 in. (43 cm).

ATLANTIC BRIEF SQUID   *Lolliguncula brevis*

Distinctly rounded fins less than half the length of mantle. Feeds on wide array of small fish. **Range:** Inshore from Delaware Bay south. **Size:** Mantle to 5 in. (12.5 cm).

GLAUCUS   *Glaucus* spp.

Nearly transparent invertebrate drifter in ocean's upper layer. Often found in debris and floating vegetation. **Range:** Northern Atlantic. **Size:** Mantle to 1.5 in. (30 mm).

GREATER ARGONAUT (PAPER NAUTILUS)   *Argonauta argo*

Elegant shelled drifter of deep seas. Best known through beautiful "paper shell" that washes up on beaches, actually an egg case secreted by female's modified arms. Male shell-less. **Range:** Warm tropical waters north to Cape Cod. **Size:** Mantle to 12 in. (30 cm).

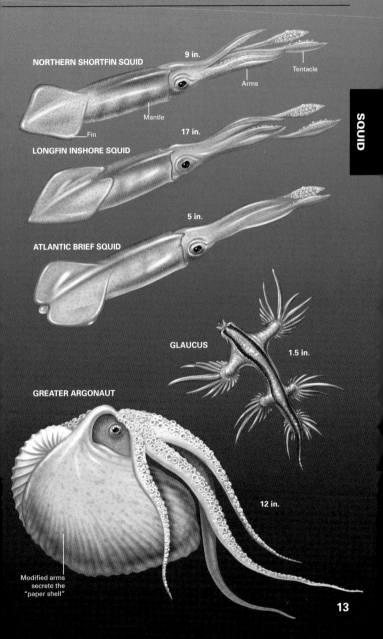

SQUID

NORTHERN SHORTFIN SQUID

9 in.

Tentacle

Arms

Mantle

Fin

LONGFIN INSHORE SQUID

17 in.

ATLANTIC BRIEF SQUID

5 in.

GLAUCUS

1.5 in.

GREATER ARGONAUT

12 in.

Modified arms
secrete the
"paper shell"

PELAGIC CRUSTACEANS

NORTHERN SHRIMP (BOREAL RED SHRIMP)   *Pandalus* spp.

Red or pink. The edible shrimp taken in Gulf of Maine fishing. Long, toothed rostrum as long or longer than carapace. First leg unclawed; second leg has tiny claws. Three species: *P. borealis,* south to Cape Cod; *P. montagui,* south to Long Island; and *P. propinquus,* south to Delmarva Peninsula. **Size:** To 5 in. (12.5 cm).

EDIBLE *PENAEUS* SHRIMP   *Penaeus* spp.

Three principal species of *Penaeus* shrimp support the Atlantic commercial shrimp fishery: Brown Shrimp, *P. aztecus,* north to Cape Cod; White Shrimp, *P. setiferus,* north to Long Island; and Pink Shrimp, *P. duorarum,* north to Delaware. All have claws on first three legs and short rostrums with teeth on both top and bottom edges. **Size:** To 8 in. (20 cm).

SLENDER SARGASSUM SHRIMP
(GULFWEED SHRIMP)   *Latreutes fucorum*

A *tiny* shrimp often found in great numbers within or around floating mats of Gulfweed. Found well offshore, typically in warmer Gulf Stream waters. Exact color highly variable, depending on surrounding environment. **Size:** 0.75 in. (20 mm).

NORTHERN SHRIMP

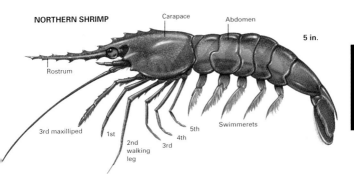

Carapace

Abdomen

5 in.

Rostrum

3rd maxilliped

1st

2nd
walking
leg

3rd

4th

5th

Swimmerets

SHRIMP

EDIBLE *PENAEUS* SHRIMP

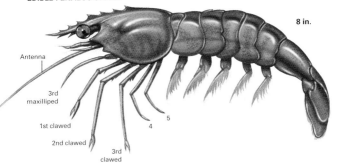

8 in.

Antenna

3rd
maxilliped

1st clawed

2nd clawed

3rd
clawed

4

5

SLENDER SARGASSUM SHRIMP

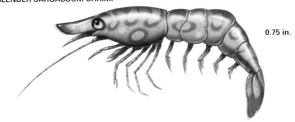

0.75 in.

15

MACKEREL SHARKS, BLUE SHARK

WHITE SHARK
Carcharodon carcharias

Conical snout, unmarked dorsal fin, and single caudal peduncle. Back color varies from slate gray to blue or dark brown. May show black spot in axil of pectoral fin. Adults of huge girth, heavier than other sharks of similar length. Known to attack humans. **Range:** All temperate waters, but rare. **Size:** To 25 ft. (7.6 m), but most under 16 ft. (4.9 m). Red List – **Vulnerable**

PORBEAGLE
Lamna nasus

Bluish above with sharp contrast to white underparts. Short, rounded rostrum. Note double-keeled peduncle. Heavily fished for its liver. **Range:** New Jersey and north in cold waters. **Size:** To 10 ft. (3 m). Red List – **Near threatened**

SHORTFIN MAKO
Isurus oxyrhinchus

Beautiful steel blue, contrasting to white underparts. Very slender with elongate snout and high upper caudal fin. Elongate peduncle keel. Pectoral fin short. Mainly pelagic. Often leaps from water in pursuit of prey. **Range:** Cape Cod to Argentina. **Size:** To 12 ft. (3.7 m). Red List – **Near threatened**

LONGFIN MAKO
Isurus paucus

Separated from look-alike Shortfin Mako by dark underparts except for white belly area. Pectoral fin longer and more swept back. A deep-water hunter until evening, when it rises to cool surface waters. **Range:** North Carolina to Cuba. **Size:** To 12 ft. (3.7 m).

BLUE SHARK
Prionace glauca

A spectacular shimmering blue shark with pure white underparts. Long, pointed snout. Very long pectoral fins. Long, graceful. Known to attack humans. **Range:** Nova Scotia and Grand Banks to Argentina. **Size:** To 12.5 ft. (3.8 m). Red List – **Near threatened**

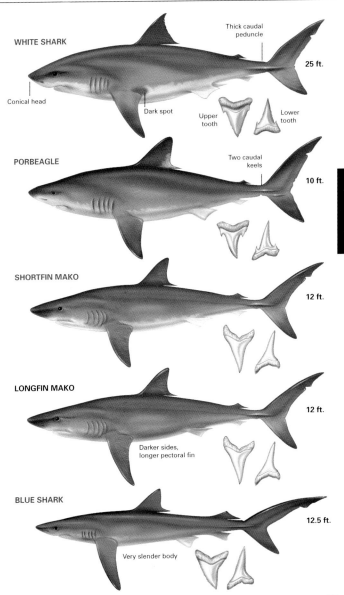

WHITE SHARK

Thick caudal peduncle

25 ft.

Conical head

Dark spot

Upper tooth

Lower tooth

PORBEAGLE

Two caudal keels

10 ft.

SHORTFIN MAKO

12 ft.

LONGFIN MAKO

12 ft.

Darker sides, longer pectoral fin

BLUE SHARK

12.5 ft.

Very slender body

SHARKS

17

LARGE PELAGIC SHARKS

These are true pelagic species that favor deeper waters. The Tiger Shark will also come into very shallow areas. The Tiger Shark and Oceanic Whitetip Shark are considered very dangerous to humans.

OCEANIC WHITETIP SHARK *Carcharhinus longimanus*

Warm brown with creamy underparts. White fin tips make this shark easy to identify. A deep-water shark in temperate waters, coming in to reefs and inshore only in tropical waters. Very dangerous. **Range:** Cape Cod to Uruguay. **Size:** To 12 ft. (3.7 m). Red List – Near threatened

TIGER SHARK *Galeocerdo cuvier*

Brownish to blue-gray with distinctive dark blotches and barring. Blunt snout. Usually pelagic and solitary. Often comes into bays at night to feed. Very dangerous. **Range:** Cape Cod to the tropics, but uncommon north of Florida. **Size:** May reach huge size, to 24 ft. (7.3 m). Red List – Near threatened

SILKY ("SICKLE") SHARK *Carcharhinus falciformis*

A slender, bluish gray shark with contrasting underparts. Note fairly small dorsal. Pectoral fin very large and streamlined. Named for its remarkably smooth skin. Primarily a deep water species, sometimes quite numerous. **Range:** Cape Cod to Brazil. **Size:** To 12 ft. (3.7 m).

BLACKTIP SHARK *Carcharhinus limbatus*

Grayish blue above, pale below. Dorsal, anal, and lower caudal fins tipped with black. Inside of pectoral tips dark. White flank patch. Pelagic but often follows schools of mackerel inshore. **Range:** Cape Cod to Brazil. **Size:** To 8 ft. (2.4 m). Red List – Near threatened

SPINNER SHARK *Carcharhinus brevipinna*

Very similar in every aspect to Blacktip Shark. But dorsal fin more to rear, snout much more elongate, and flank patch merely a white line, not a patch. Erupts from the water with spectacular spinning leaps reminiscent of Sailfish breaking the ocean surface. **Range:** North Carolina to Brazil. **Size:** To 10 ft. (3 m). Red List – Near threatened

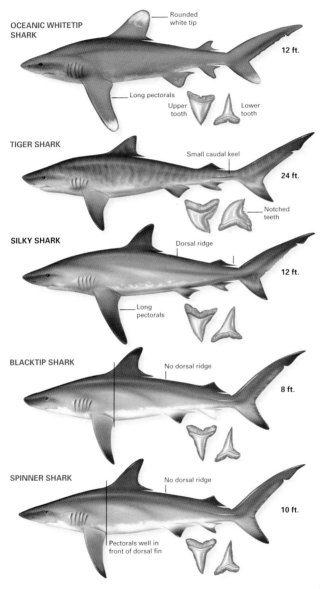

OCEANIC WHITETIP SHARK
- Rounded white tip
- 12 ft.
- Long pectorals
- Upper tooth
- Lower tooth

TIGER SHARK
- Small caudal keel
- 24 ft.
- Notched teeth

SILKY SHARK
- Dorsal ridge
- 12 ft.
- Long pectorals

BLACKTIP SHARK
- No dorsal ridge
- 8 ft.

SPINNER SHARK
- No dorsal ridge
- 10 ft.
- Pectorals well in front of dorsal fin

SHARKS

19

PILOTFISH, REMORAS

Pilotfish are free-swimming fish that prefer to live in association with large sharks or other predatory fish. They are also commonly found under floating mats of Gulfweed. Pilotfish do not have sucker disks and never attach themselves to their hosts. Remoras and sharksuckers directly attach themselves to large sharks, Manta Rays, and large bony fish, feeding on scraps of their hosts' dinners and taking smaller fish not eaten by the host. Sharksuckers sometimes attach themselves to human swimmers – the encounters are startling but harmless.

PILOTFISH   *Naucrates ductor*

Flanks boldly marked with five to seven dark bands. Caudal peduncle shows a small, fleshy keel. Swims freely, in association with large sharks, Mantas, or large fish. Also commonly seen under floating Gulfweed rafts. Body very rough and scaly to the touch. **Range:** Deep ocean waters worldwide. **Size:** To 27 in. (69 cm).

REMORA   *Remora remora*

Elongated body and flattened head with oval sucking disk. Lower jaw projects past upper jaw. Body color brown to dark brown. Attaches mainly to larger sharks, but may attach to any large ray, fish, or turtle. **Range:** Nova Scotia through tropics, usually in deeper waters. **Size:** To 30 in. (76 cm).

SHARKSUCKER   *Echeneis naucrates*

Elongated body very similar in shape and size to Remora. Colors vary, but always a wide, dark stripe down center of sides, bounded by thinner white stripes on top and bottom. Will often swim free of hosts, but prefers to attach itself to large fish, sharks, or turtles. Often caught by fishers in shallow coastal waters. **Range:** Nova Scotia through tropics. **Size:** To 36 in. (91 cm).

WHITEFIN SHARKSUCKER   *Echeneis neucratoides*

Very similar to Sharksucker, but with extensive white areas in dorsal, anal, and tail fins. White stripes above and below dark central stripe very prominent. Will often swim free of hosts, but prefers to attach to large fish, sharks, or turtles. Much less common than Sharksucker. **Range:** Nova Scotia through tropics. **Size:** To 30 in. (76 cm).

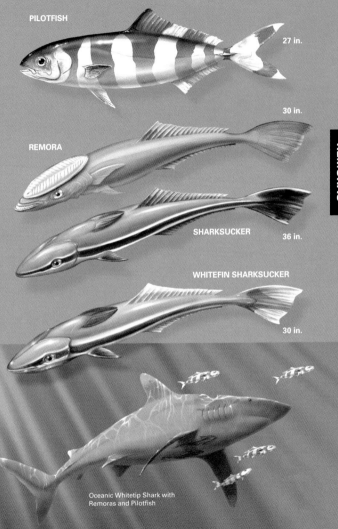

PILOTFISH

27 in.

REMORA

30 in.

SHARKSUCKER   36 in.

WHITEFIN SHARKSUCKER

30 in.

Oceanic Whitetip Shark with
Remoras and Pilotfish

SANDBAR SHARK (BROWN SHARK)   *Carcharhinus plumbeus*

Dark gray to brown and very pale below. Very high dorsal fin. Most
common shark in shallower coastal waters. Enters bays with muddy
bottoms. Migrates south in schools during late fall, when most bay
sightings are made. **Range:** Massachusetts to Brazil. More common
north of Cape Hatteras. **Size:** To 10 ft. (3 m). Red List – LR, Conservation
dependent

DUSKY SHARK   *Carcharhinus obscurus*

Dark gray to brownish. Long, rounded snout. Distinct mid-dorsal
ridge between small dorsal fins. Very large eyes. Mainly pelagic but
occasionally wanders into coastal waters and river mouths. **Range:**
Georges Bank to Brazil. **Size:** To 12 ft. (3.7 m). Red List – LR, Conservation
dependent

BULL SHARK   *Carcharhinus leucas*

A large-bodied shark with a short snout. Gray to muddy brown-white
below. No mid-dorsal ridge. One of the most common large sharks.
Very dangerous and known to attack humans. Common in coastal and
offshore waters. **Range:** Massachusetts to Brazil. **Size:** To 12 ft. (3.7 m).
Red List – LR, Conservation dependent

SAND TIGER (SAND SHARK)   *Carcharias taurus*

Grayish brown to tan. A common shark of coastal waters. Often hunts
in groups and in such shallow waters that its back is well exposed.
When feeding at the surface often expels air through gills, creating a
sound like a whale spouting. **Range:** Atlantic Coast from Gulf of Maine
to northern Florida. **Size:** To 10.5 ft. (3.2 m). Red List – LR, Conservation
dependent

NURSE SHARK   *Ginglymostoma cirratum*

Rusty to yellowish brown. Note barbel on side of each nostril, used to
locate shellfish and crustaceans. Rounded dorsal fin positioned far
back over pelvic fin. Prefers coastal waters and bays. Likes reefs. **Range:**
As far north as Rhode Island but more common south from North
Carolina. **Size:** To 14 ft. (4.3 m). Red List – LR, Conservation dependent

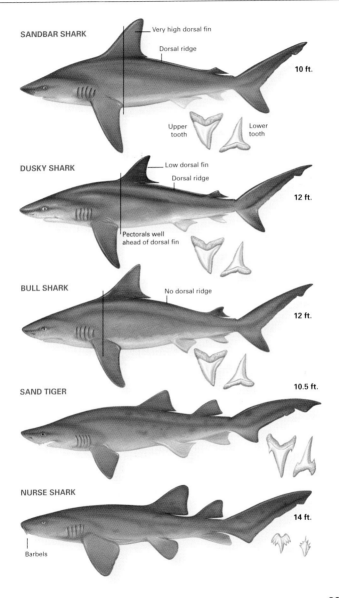

SANDBAR SHARK
Very high dorsal fin
Dorsal ridge
10 ft.
Upper tooth
Lower tooth

DUSKY SHARK
Low dorsal fin
Dorsal ridge
12 ft.
Pectorals well ahead of dorsal fin

BULL SHARK
No dorsal ridge
12 ft.

SAND TIGER
10.5 ft.

NURSE SHARK
14 ft.
Barbels

SHARKS

23

THRESHER SHARKS, HAMMERHEADS

THRESHER SHARK
Alopias vulpinus

An extraordinarily long upper caudal fin is diagnostic of threshers and separates these large sharks from all others. Brownish to gray-brown. Normal eye size. **Range:** Gulf of St. Lawrence to Florida. Occurs off North Atlantic coast mainly in summer. **Size:** To 20 ft. (6.1 m). **Red List – Data deficient**

BIGEYE THRESHER
Alopias superciliosus

Appearance like Thresher Shark, but note very large eyes, positioned high on head to allow shark to view upward. Back humped, dorsal fin set far back. **Range:** North to New York. **Size:** To 18 ft. (5.5 m).

BONNETHEAD SHARK
Sphyrna tiburo

Grayish shark with flattened head in form of shovel with eyes at edge of expanded portion. Abundant in bays and shallows into estuaries. **Range:** North to Cape Cod. **Size:** To 6 ft. (1.8 m).

SMOOTH HAMMERHEAD
Sphyrna zygaena

Almost identical to Scalloped Hammerhead, but without indentation in forehead and black tip on pectoral fin. **Range:** North to Nova Scotia in summer. **Size:** To 13 ft. (4 m). **Red List – Data deficient**

SCALLOPED HAMMERHEAD
Sphyrna lewini

Light brown or gray above, pale below. Note convex forehead with distinct indentation in front. Pectorals black on inside tips. Enters bays and shallow waters. **Range:** North to Nova Scotia. **Size:** To 10 ft. (3 m). **Red List – Data deficient**

GREAT HAMMERHEAD
Sphyrna mokarran

The largest and most pelagic and tropical of the hammerheads. Front edge of head slightly indented, giving head very square appearance. Back edge of pelvic fin very curved. **Range:** North Carolina to Brazil; tropical waters worldwide. **Size:** To 20 ft. (6.1 m). **Red List – Data deficient**

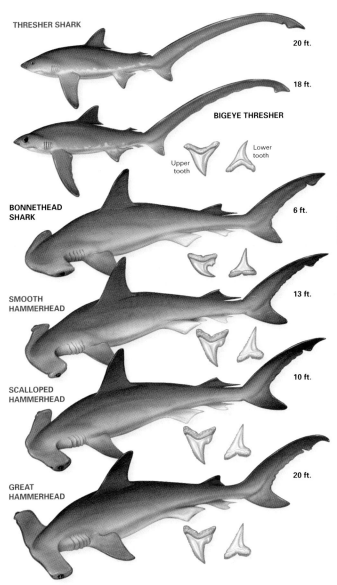

THRESHER SHARK

20 ft.

18 ft.

BIGEYE THRESHER

Lower tooth

Upper tooth

BONNETHEAD SHARK

6 ft.

SMOOTH HAMMERHEAD

13 ft.

SCALLOPED HAMMERHEAD

10 ft.

GREAT HAMMERHEAD

20 ft.

SHARKS

UNUSUAL SHARKS, DOGFISH

SIXGILL SHARK
Hexanchus griseus

Single dorsal fin, very long dorsal lobe of caudal fin, and six gill slits. Prefers deep warm waters, surfacing at night to feed. Uncommon; habits poorly known. **Range:** North Carolina through Gulf of Mexico. **Size:** To 16 ft. (4.9 m). **Red List – Near threatened**

GREENLAND SHARK
Somniosus microcephalus

Very large brown or gray shark with two low dorsal fins. Unusual shape for a large shark; essentially a giant dogfish. First dorsal fin originates well toward rear, about halfway between nose and tail. Flesh poisonous. **Range:** Greenland to Gulf of Maine. **Size:** To 22 ft. (6.7 m).

PORTUGUESE SHARK
Centroscymnus coelolepis

Small, dark brown shark with two very low dorsal fins. Favors deep, cold waters well offshore. **Range:** Grand Banks and Newfoundland to New York. **Size:** To 3.5 ft. (1.1 m).

SPINY DOGFISH
Squalus acanthias

Very small brown to gray shark with spotted flanks. Both dorsal fins show prominent spines at leading edges. Very common; often swims in large schools. Not fished commercially in our area, but popular in Europe as the main species served in "fish and chips." **Range:** Newfoundland to North Carolina. **Size:** To 4 ft. (1.2 m).

SMOOTH DOGFISH
Mustelus canis

Very small, slender dogfish *without* spines along leading edges of either dorsal fin. Prominent spiracle opening behind eye. Enters bays in northern waters; prefers deeper, cooler water in southern parts of range. Very common; often caught by sportfishers. **Range:** Bay of Fundy to Uruguay. **Size:** To 5 ft. (1.5 m).

BLACK DOGFISH
Centroscyllium fabricii

Small, dark brown dogfish with black belly and prominent spines forward of both dorsal fins. Second dorsal fin larger than first. Older specimens may be black throughout. Very common in northern parts of range, preferring deep, cold waters. **Range:** Southern Greenland to Virginia. **Size:** To 3.5 ft. (1.1 m).

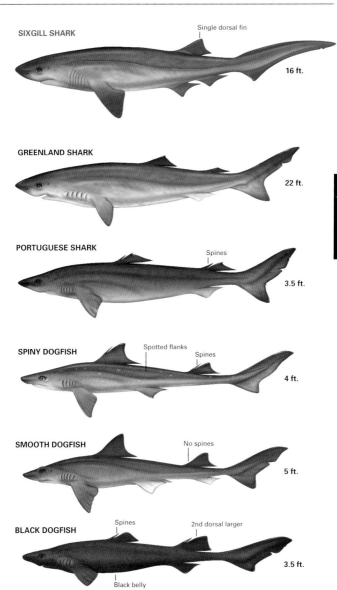

SIXGILL SHARK

Single dorsal fin

16 ft.

GREENLAND SHARK

22 ft.

SHARKS

PORTUGUESE SHARK

Spines

3.5 ft.

SPINY DOGFISH

Spotted flanks

Spines

4 ft.

SMOOTH DOGFISH

No spines

5 ft.

BLACK DOGFISH

Spines

2nd dorsal larger

3.5 ft.

Black belly

27

Description: A huge brown or slate-gray shark with gigantic mouth and very long gill slits that extend from its back to near midline of throat. Massive lunate tail with large caudal keels. Teeth tiny. The second largest fish after Whale Shark. Gill slits extremely long, nearly circling head. A filter feeder like baleen whales. Special baleen-like extensions of gill arches called "rakes" filter planktonic animals from water. **Red List – Vulnerable**

Habits: A docile and sluggish swimmer, not known to harm swimmers or boats. Sometimes aggregates in groups and may swim head-to-toe in lines of six to eight individuals. Although reasonably common, its natural history is not well known. In winter disappears from surface waters, moving into deep waters offshore.

Range: Newfoundland to North Carolina; temperate waters worldwide. Prefers cold, upwelling waters where plankton is richest, migrating south along east coast in winter, then north again in summer.

Size: Huge; a 30-ft. (9.1-m) specimen can weigh 8,600 lbs. (3,900 kg). Basking Sharks may reach 32 ft. (9.7 m) in length, but most individuals in our area average 22–29 ft. (6.7–8.8 m) or smaller.

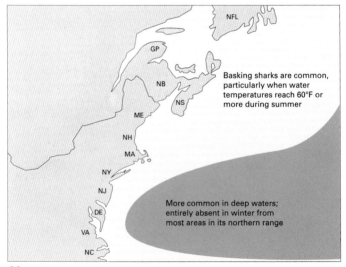

Basking sharks are common, particularly when water temperatures reach 60°F or more during summer

More common in deep waters; entirely absent in winter from most areas in its northern range

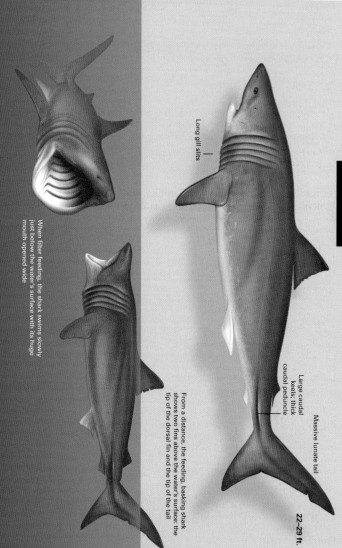

SHARKS

Long gill slits

When filter feeding, the shark swims slowly just below the water's surface with its huge mouth opened wide

From a distance, the feeding, basking shark shows two fins above the water's surface: the tip of the dorsal fin and the tip of the tail

Large caudal keels; thick caudal peduncle

Massive lunate tail

22–29 ft.

WHALE SHARK

Rhincodon typus

Description: A huge, gray, bluish, or greenish shark with mottled pattern of light spots throughout back and sides. Three pronounced ridges run along both sides of back, merging into prominent caudal keels on either side of tail. Head very wide, with terminal mouth. The largest living fish. **Red List – Vulnerable**

Habits: A slow-swimming surface filter feeder. Though uncommon throughout our area, it is easily observed if found. Usually solitary, but sometimes aggregates into groups in tropical waters. Like Basking Shark, feeds just below the water's surface, but its dorsal and tail fins often do not break the surface. Generally docile; often ridden by divers who grab onto its dorsal fins or back ridges. Sometimes reported to ram boats, more likely the boats rammed the sharks.

Range: New York through Caribbean; warmer temperate and tropical waters worldwide. Sporadic reports of sightings north of Cape Cod.

Size: Largest measured specimen 40 ft. (12.2 m) and 26,594 lbs. (12,063 kg), but numerous reliable reports of individuals to 60 ft. (18.3 m).

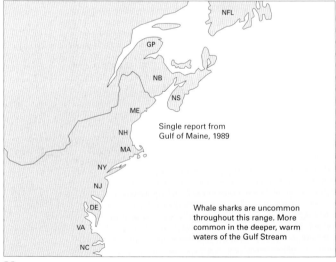

Single report from Gulf of Maine, 1989

Whale sharks are uncommon throughout this range. More common in the deeper, warm waters of the Gulf Stream

Very wide
terminal mouth

Three ridges on back

Thick caudal keels

SHARKS

25–30 ft.

PELAGIC RAYS

Pelagic rays are more common well offshore in warmer waters, but they do enter coastal waters. Atlantic Mantas often cruise offshore channel areas and the outer reaches of reefs, feeding on plankton. Mantas and Spotted Eagle Rays are generally solitary, whereas Devil Rays often appear in schools. Mantas may breach spontaneously near boats, and all the larger rays may leap from the ocean surface if pursued.

ATLANTIC MANTA (DEVILFISH) *Manta birostris*

The largest ray, can reach giant size. Disc black above, almost twice as wide as long, often showing gray or whitish patches near shoulders. Undersurface ranges from black or gray to almost white. Prominent cephalic fins, or "horns," flank terminal mouth (at leading edge of disc, not recessed as in Devil Ray). Often seen at or just below the water's surface. Harmless unless attacked or tangled in fishing or boating gear. **Range:** Cape Cod to Brazil. **Size:** Width to 22 ft. (6.7 m). Red List – Data deficient

DEVIL RAY *Mobula hypostoma*

Very similar to small Atlantic Manta. Disc black above, white or light gray below. Mouth subterminal rather than terminal as in similar Manta. Tail length equals body length, proportionately much longer than Manta's relatively short tail. Travels in schools. **Range:** Warm southern waters to Brazil; rarely as far north as New Jersey in summer. **Size:** Width to 4 ft. (1.2 m).

SPOTTED EAGLE RAY *Myliobatus aquila*

Disc blue-gray, gray, or brown above, with lighter spots varying in size and shape. Head distinct from body. Tail very long and whip-like, with two spines at base. Favors shallow coastal waters; often seen in bays, inlets, and estuaries. **Range:** North to Cape Hatteras in summer; tropical waters worldwide. **Size:** Width to 8 ft. (2.4 m). Red List – Data deficient

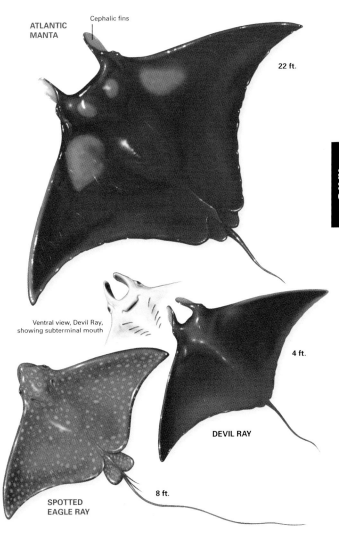

ATLANTIC MANTA

Cephalic fins

22 ft.

RAYS

Ventral view, Devil Ray, showing subterminal mouth

4 ft.

DEVIL RAY

SPOTTED EAGLE RAY

8 ft.

PUFFERS, PORCUPINEFISH

These fish are named for their unusual habit of swallowing water or air to increase their size and thereby deter predators from swallowing them. Most puffers cannot be eaten owing to the presence of a neurotoxin known as tetrodotoxin in their flesh.

NORTHERN PUFFER   *Sphoeroides maculatus*

Olive-gray with many black dots speckled over upper side. Black band between eyes. Fins usually yellowish, with yellow edging on dark side stripes. A fish of inshore waters, harbors, and estuaries. Nontoxic and sold as "sea squab." **Range:** Cape Cod to Florida. **Size:** To 14 in. (36 cm).

SMOOTH PUFFER   *Lagocephalus laevigatus*

Bluish gray overall, with indistinct broad banding (bands more distinct in young specimens). No spines. Forked caudal fin. Mainly pelagic. Adults are seen at the ocean's surface far offshore. Young are more common inshore on coastal banks. **Range:** Cape Cod to Argentina. **Size:** To 24 in. (61 cm).

OCEANIC PUFFER   *Lagocephalus lagocephalus*

Similar to Smooth and Northern Puffers, but darker blue above, with contrasting white undersurface. When viewed floating in surface waters, note how close dorsal fin is to caudal. As its name suggests, this is the most pelagic of the puffers, and healthy adults are rarely encountered in inshore waters. **Range:** Nova Scotia to Florida. **Size:** To 24 in. (61 cm).

PORCUPINEFISH   *Diodon hystrix*

Yellowish tan body covered with spines that can be elevated. Numerous small spots on body. Large eyes. Similar to smaller Balloonfish (*D. holocanthus*), but spines on forehead shorter than those on body. **Range:** Mainly southern waters, but drifts north in Gulf Stream. **Size:** To 36 in. (91 cm).

SPOTTED BURRFISH   *Chilomycterus atringa*

Similar to small Porcupinefish. Yellowish tan body with very short spines that appear triangular in cross-section. Note distinct black spotting on back and fine spotting covering all fins. **Range:** North in warm offshore waters to Nova Scotia, but very uncommon north of Cape Hatteras. **Size:** To 18 in. (46 cm).

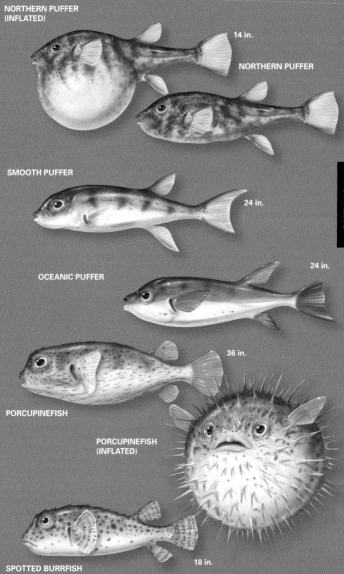

NORTHERN PUFFER
(INFLATED)

14 in.

NORTHERN PUFFER

SMOOTH PUFFER

24 in.

OCEANIC PUFFER

24 in.

36 in.

PORCUPINEFISH

PORCUPINEFISH
(INFLATED)

SPOTTED BURRFISH

18 in.

PUFFERS

HERRING, SHAD, MENHADEN

A large family of some 27 species that have long been staples of the fishing industry. As with many ocean fish, overfishing has contributed to declining populations.

AMERICAN SHAD *Alosa sapidissima*

Extremely laterally compressed with dark back and silvery sides showing a row of spots on upper portion. Known for famous "shad runs" up large rivers such as the Connecticut River. **Range:** New Brunswick to Florida. **Size:** To 30 in. (76 cm).

ATLANTIC MENHADEN (MOSSBUNKER) *Brevoortia tyrannus*

Small version of American Shad, with distinctly larger head in proportion to body. Occurs in large schools that support an east coast fishery producing fish oil for market. **Range:** New Brunswick to Florida. **Size:** To 18 in. (46 cm).

HICKORY SHAD *Alosa mediocris*

Nearly identical to American Shad, but mouth turns distinctly upward and side spotting starts right next to gill cover. Dark blue back. During "shad runs" up rivers can become infected with water molds that produce large lesions. **Range:** Maine to Florida. **Size:** To 26 in. (66 cm).

ATLANTIC HERRING *Clupea harengus*

Elongate silver fish, less laterally flattened than most in family. Occurs in massive schools that frequent the open ocean surface. Taken by large fisheries, they are also taken by offshore fishing boats and provide food for whales and larger sport fish. **Range:** Greenland to North Carolina. **Size:** To 18 in. (46 cm).

BLUEBACK HERRING *Alosa aestivalis*

Very similar to Alewife in color patterns and behavior. Mixes with shad and Alewifes during runs. Bluebacks have smaller eye and more blue-green back but can be hard to separate from similar herrings. **Range:** Nova Scotia to Florida. **Size:** To 14 in. (36 cm).

ALEWIFE *Alosa pseudoharengus*

Strongly dorsally compressed with a blue-black back and silvery sides. Moves in incredible numbers – called Alewife runs – from coastal and estuarine areas to inland breeding sites. Important food species for Striped Bass, Bluefish, and other sport fish. **Range:** Newfoundland to South Carolina. **Size:** To 15 in. (38 cm).

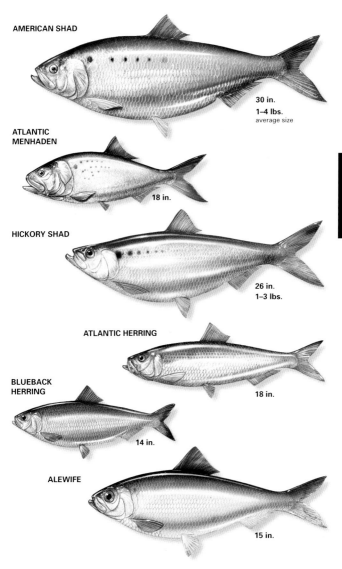

AMERICAN SHAD

30 in.
1–4 lbs.
average size

ATLANTIC
MENHADEN

18 in.

HICKORY SHAD

26 in.
1–3 lbs.

ATLANTIC HERRING

18 in.

BLUEBACK
HERRING

14 in.

ALEWIFE

15 in.

HERRING

CODS

No family of fish is more closely linked with the fishing industry of the Northwestern Atlantic. The Atlantic Cod and its close relatives have been the staple of east coast diets for 400 years. Once considered to be endlessly abundant, the Atlantic Cod has been depleted by overfishing.

ATLANTIC COD   *Gadus morhua*

A bottom-dwelling fish of deep waters. Brownish to olive-green, heavily spotted. Note chin barbel. The population is overfished, and cod are declining rapidly all along the east coast. Weight now averages less than 20 lbs. (9 kg), although past specimens sometimes reached 200 lbs. (91 kg). **Range:** Greenland to North Carolina. **Size:** Typically 12–24 in. (30–61 cm). **Red List – Vulnerable**

POLLOCK   *Pollachius virens*

Slimmer than a cod, this greenish olive relative with protruding lower jaw lacks a noticeable chin barbel. Fast swimmers, Pollock will school to capture other fish and will come to the surface to feed. **Range:** Newfoundland to North Carolina, with greatest concentrations in Gulf of Maine. **Size:** To 35 in. (89 cm).

HADDOCK   *Melanogrammus aeglefinus*

An excellent food fish of cool, deep waters. Note dark spot above pectoral fin. **Range:** Newfoundland to North Carolina; more common in northern range. **Size:** Typically to 24 in. (61 cm). **Red List – Vulnerable**

SILVER HAKE   *Merluccius bilinearis*

A trim silver fish with protruding lower jaw and lacking typical cod chin barbel. Rear dorsal and anal fins almost mirror of each other in shape. Travels in small groups, attacking prey fish in a feeding frenzy. Populations split into northern and southern stocks. **Range:** Newfoundland to North Carolina. **Size:** To 30 in. (76 cm).

WHITE HAKE   *Urophycis tenuis*

Elongate, whisker-like ventral fins separate this fish from others in group. These long fins are used for hunting in the dark in deep, cold waters for crabs and mollusks. **Range:** Newfoundland to Cape Hatteras. **Size:** To 48 in. (1.2 m).

CUSK   *Brosme brosme*

Elongated single dorsal and anal fins. Note chin barbel. A fish of cold, deep waters, often accidentally hooked by cod fishers in deep waters of Gulf of Maine. Feeds mostly on lobsters, other crustaceans, and smaller bottom-dwelling fish. Good eating, and a valuable market fish. **Range:** Newfoundland to New Jersey. **Size:** To 35 in. (89 cm).

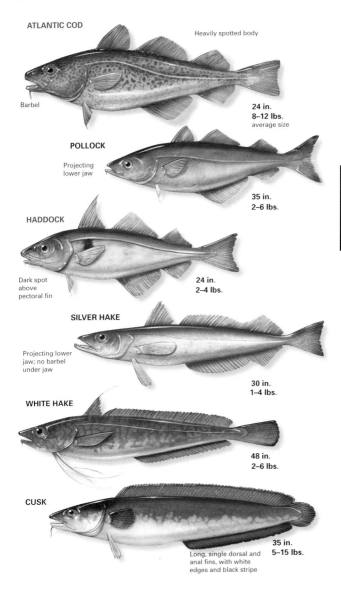

ATLANTIC COD

Heavily spotted body

Barbel

24 in.
8–12 lbs.
average size

POLLOCK

Projecting
lower jaw

35 in.
2–6 lbs.

HADDOCK

Dark spot
above
pectoral fin

24 in.
2–4 lbs.

SILVER HAKE

Projecting lower
jaw; no barbel
under jaw

30 in.
1–4 lbs.

WHITE HAKE

48 in.
2–6 lbs.

CUSK

35 in.
5–15 lbs.

Long, single dorsal and
anal fins, with white
edges and black stripe

FLYINGFISH

This group favors tropical offshore waters. The species below frequent the Gulf Stream, and a few can be found in open temperate oceans. Flyingfish sometimes enter inshore waters after storms but are generally seen in warm offshore waters.

OCEANIC TWO-WING FLYINGFISH   *Exocoetus obtusirostris*

Very long pectoral fins, blunt head. Dorsal fin small and unmarked. The only two-winged flyingfish to reach our area. **Range:** New Jersey south, far offshore or in Gulf Stream. **Size:** To 10 in. (25 cm).

MARGINED FLYINGFISH   *Cypselurus cyanopterus*

Pectoral fins and caudal fin uniformly dusky. Large dark patch along upper edge of dorsal fin. **Range:** New Jersey south, far offshore or in Gulf Stream. **Size:** To 18 in. (46 cm).

BANDWING FLYINGFISH   *Cheilopogon exsiliens*

Spectacular dark blue pectoral fins with narrow, clear crossing bands. Caudal fin clear on top and dusky on lower portion. Common offshore. **Range:** Cape Cod south, far offshore or in Gulf Stream. **Size:** To 12 in. (31 cm).

ATLANTIC FLYINGFISH   *Cheilopogon melanurus*

Black pectoral fins with clear central area. Dusky caudal fin. The most common flyingfish of Gulf Stream waters. Often seen skittering away from the bow of boats in deep offshore waters. Very common in southern waters off Florida; unusual in northern waters. **Range:** Cape Cod south, far offshore or in Gulf Stream. **Size:** To 16 in. (41 cm).

SPOTFIN FLYINGFISH   *Cheilopogon furcatus*

Striking black pectoral fins with wide, clear crossing bands. Pelvic fins with dark tips and caudals clear. Commonly enters bays and shallow coastal waters in Florida and Gulf of Mexico. **Range:** Cape Cod south, far offshore or in Gulf Stream. **Size:** To 14 in. (36 cm).

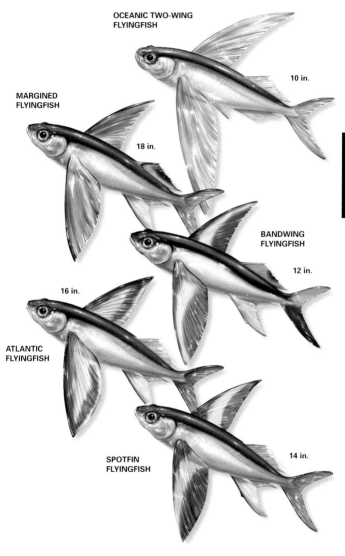

OCEANIC TWO-WING
FLYINGFISH

10 in.

MARGINED
FLYINGFISH

18 in.

BANDWING
FLYINGFISH

12 in.

16 in.

ATLANTIC
FLYINGFISH

SPOTFIN
FLYINGFISH

14 in.

FLYINGFISH

POMPANOS, JACKS

Pompanos are swift, nervous inshore predators. They make delicious eating but are challenging to hook. Jacks are voracious offshore game fish often found near reefs and structures in deeper waters.

PERMIT   *Trachinotus falcatus*

Large, silvery, disk-shaped fish. Note swept-back dorsal and anal fins. Dark blotch near pectoral usually distinctive. **Range:** Massachusetts to Brazil. **Weight:** To 50 lbs. (23 kg). **Size:** To 45 in. (1.1 m).

FLORIDA POMPANO   *Trachinotus carolinus*

Very similar to Permit, but lacks dark blotch on flank. Back often blue-black. Common in coastal bays and estuaries. An important food fish. **Range:** Massachusetts to Brazil. **Weight:** To 8 lbs. (3.6 kg). **Size:** To 25 in. (64 cm).

AFRICAN POMPANO   *Alectis ciliaris*

Rays of dorsal and anal fins reduced to distinctive thread-like projections. Young specimens, called "threadfish," have fin projections much longer than body. Note very steep forehead angle. **Range:** Massachusetts to Brazil. **Weight:** To 40 lbs. (18 kg). **Size:** To 45 in. (1.1 m).

YELLOW JACK   *Carangoides bartholomaei*

Forehead sloped compared to other jacks. Dark back with yellowish underparts. An excellent sport fish. **Range:** Massachusetts to Brazil. **Weight:** To 17 lbs. (8 kg). **Size:** To 39 in. (1 m).

HORSE-EYE JACK   *Caranx latus*

Silvery with black spot on operculum but not on pectoral fin. Large eye. Yellowish caudal fin. **Range:** New Jersey to Bermuda along Atlantic Coast. **Weight:** To 8 lbs. (3.6 kg). **Size:** To 30 in. (75 cm).

CREVALLE JACK   *Caranx hippos*

Large, deep bodied, with blunt forehead. Distinct spots on operculum and pectoral fin separate Crevalle Jack from other jacks. Important food and game fish. **Range:** Nova Scotia to Uruguay. **Weight:** To 20 lbs. (9 kg). **Size:** To 60 in. (1.5 m).

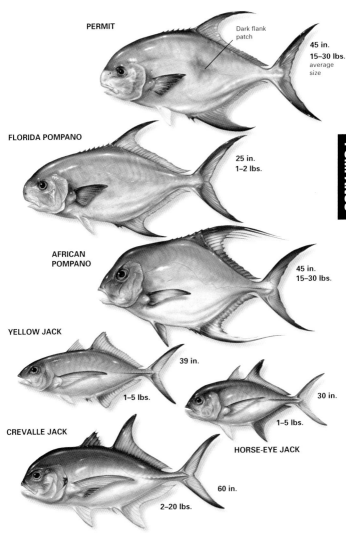

PERMIT

Dark flank patch

45 in.
15–30 lbs.
average size

FLORIDA POMPANO

25 in.
1–2 lbs.

AFRICAN POMPANO

45 in.
15–30 lbs.

YELLOW JACK

39 in.

1–5 lbs.

30 in.

1–5 lbs.

CREVALLE JACK

HORSE-EYE JACK

60 in.

2–20 lbs.

DOLPHINS, LOUVAR, OPAH

Dolphins are colorful pelagic predators that are highly prized for their delicious meat. They are often found near or under floating debris or Gulfweed mats. Louvars and Opahs are unusual solitary pelagic fish.

DOLPHIN (DORADO) *Coryphaena hippurus*

Brilliant coloration of greenish blues with gold flecking. Very steep forehead in male (bull). Swift swimmer, hunting in "packs." Feeds on fish and squid. Attracted to floating debris under which it feeds. Excellent eating. This is the Mahi-Mahi of Hawaii. **Range:** Nova Scotia to Brazil. **Size:** To 7 ft. (2.1 m).

POMPANO DOLPHIN *Coryphaena equiselis*

Separated from very similar male Dolphin by smaller size, but may be confused with young or female Dolphin. Silvery to pale yellow. Note small pectoral fin and convex (not concave) edge of anal fin. **Range:** New Jersey to Brazil. **Size:** To 7 ft. (2.1 m).

LOUVAR *Luvarus imperialis*

Flattened silver fish with red to pink fins. Steep forehead in adult. Appearance changes with age; young specimens look like puffers. May be related to tunas. Solitary, rarely seen. **Range:** Temperate waters worldwide. Prefers deep water at edge of continental shelf. **Size:** To 6 ft. (1.8 m).

OPAH *Lampris guttatus*

Almost flat, circular in form, with stiff, long pectoral fins with sharp tips. Note upward arc of lateral line above pectoral fin. Bright red fins contrast with spotted bluish-silver body. Jaws lack teeth. Important food fish in Europe. **Range:** Grand Banks to Florida. **Size:** To 6 ft. (1.8 m).

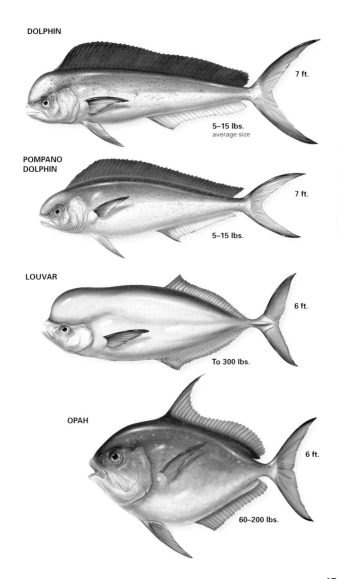

DOLPHIN

7 ft.

5–15 lbs.
average size

POMPANO
DOLPHIN

7 ft.

5–15 lbs.

LOUVAR

6 ft.

To 300 lbs.

OPAH

6 ft.

60–200 lbs.

DOLPHINS

GAME FISH

Most of these popular game fish are medium-sized predators that frequent both inshore waters and the deeper waters of the continental shelf. Populations of these species fluctuate, but most are considered to be in a long-term decline due to overfishing, pollution, and habitat loss.

GREAT BARRACUDA *Sphyraena borealis*

Large and slim. Overshot lower jaw reveals numerous sharp teeth. Large, triangular tail. Can be aggressive toward divers. Flesh edible but may cause ciguatera poisoning. **Range:** Massachusetts south; prefers warm waters. **Weight:** To over 100 lbs. (45 kg). **Size:** To 6 ft. (1.8 m).

COBIA *Rachycentron canadum*

Large, brownish, with dark side stripes and pale underparts. Lower jaw protrudes like a barracuda's, but teeth smaller. Spines form first part of dorsal fin. Hunts near floating matter and buoys. **Range:** Massachusetts to Florida. **Weight:** To 150 lbs. (68 kg). **Size:** To 6 ft. (1.8 m).

BLUEFISH *Pomatomus saltatrix*

Blue above, silver below. Jaw has numerous very sharp teeth. Hunts in schools; voracious in feeding. Will drive fish into shallow areas and attack. Bluefish have even bitten bathers when in feeding frenzies. A very important game fish. **Range:** Nova Scotia to Argentina. **Weight:** To 27 lbs. (12 kg). **Size:** To 45 in. (1.1 m).

ATLANTIC SALMON *Salmo salar*

Silvery with dark side splotches that become distinct black Xs with age. Migrates to fresh water to spawn. Adults do not die after spawning but return to ocean. Efforts to restore salmon in cleaned-up rivers are well under way. **Range:** Greenland to Long Island, formerly to New Jersey. **Weight:** To 25–80 lbs. (11–36 kg). **Size:** To 5 ft. (1.5 m).

STRIPED BASS *Morone saxatilis*

Large, swift, silvery, with seven or eight distinct dark side stripes. Very dependent on water temperature for movement in- and offshore. Important game and food fish. **Range:** Gulf of St. Lawrence to Florida. **Weight:** Rarely above 45 lbs. (20 kg) but ranges to 125 lbs. (57 kg). **Size:** To 6 ft. (1.8 m) but typically 2–3 ft. (61–91 cm).

GAME FISH

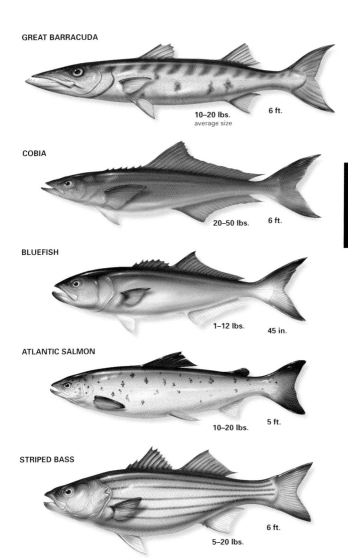

GREAT BARRACUDA

10–20 lbs.
average size

6 ft.

COBIA

20–50 lbs.

6 ft.

BLUEFISH

1–12 lbs.

45 in.

ATLANTIC SALMON

10–20 lbs.

5 ft.

STRIPED BASS

6 ft.

5–20 lbs.

GAME FISH

SMALLER GAME FISH

The northeast coastal waters are the home to a rich diversity of smaller game fish that attract offshore and inshore fishers.

BLACK SEA BASS   *Centropristis striata*

A bottom-dwelling fish, one of the most popular northeastern game fish. Unlike its relative the Striped Bass, it is strictly marine and does not enter fresh water. Stocky body with high back and sloping head; note single spine atop gill cover. Color varies greatly from gray to brown to indigo. **Range:** Resident from southern Massachusetts to Florida. **Size:** To 16 in. (41 cm).

CUNNER   *Tautogolabrus adspersus*

This good pan fish varies in color depending on where it lives: deep-water Cunners are more reddish; shallow, sandy-bottom Cunners are more olive with flecking. Common off piers and breakwaters. **Range:** Newfoundland to New Jersey and occasionally to Chesapeake Bay. **Size:** To 10 in. (25 cm).

ACADIAN REDFISH   *Sebastes fasciatus*

Use caution when handling this fish – its spines are sharp! This deep-water fish is orange to flame-red with large eyes that indicate its preference for bottom dwelling. It feeds on mollusks and small fish. **Range:** Gulf of Maine. **Size:** To 20 in. (51 cm).

SCUP (PORGY)   *Stenotomus chrysops*

Silvery to brownish, with distinct lateral line on silvery pink side. Although disdained by many offshore fishers in quest of larger fish, this common species is a good table fish. **Range:** Nova Scotia to Florida. **Size:** To 18 in. (46 cm).

TAUTOG   *Tautoga onitis*

Typical bottom-dweller, ranging widely in color. Blunt head, thick-lipped, with well-developed canine teeth in powerful jaws – beware when handling! A popular and delicious sport fish. Young specimens are spectacular green, growing under protection of abundant Sea Lettuce (*Ulva* spp.). **Range:** Nova Scotia to South Carolina. **Size:** To 36 in. (91 cm).

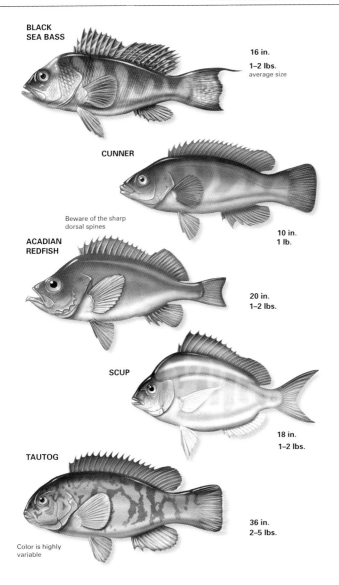

BLACK SEA BASS

16 in.
1–2 lbs.
average size

CUNNER

10 in.
1 lb.

Beware of the sharp
dorsal spines

ACADIAN REDFISH

20 in.
1–2 lbs.

SCUP

18 in.
1–2 lbs.

TAUTOG

36 in.
2–5 lbs.

Color is highly
variable

GAME FISH

INSHORE GAME, BAIT, AND PREY FISH

WHITE PERCH
Morone americana

A common species that often migrates up rivers with other fish, such as Alewife, to breed. A popular recreational and important commercial fish. **Range:** Maritime Provinces to mid-Florida coast. **Size:** To 19 in. (48 cm).

WEAKFISH
Cynoscion regalis

Populations of this favorite sport fish fluctuate in numbers and occurrence. Bone and flesh structure of mouth area allow this species to toss a hook easily from "weak" mouthparts, hence common name. **Range:** Nova Scotia to Florida. **Size:** To 20 in. (51 cm).

BALLYHOO
Hemiramphus brasiliensis

These warm-water halfbeaks (narrow-bodied fishes with elongated jaws) are related to flyingfish. Schools in large numbers near the water's surface and serves as food for larger game fish such as sailfishes, billfish, and mackerel. Harvested mainly as baitfish for offshore fishing. **Range:** New York to Brazil. **Size:** To 8 in. (21 cm).

BALAO
Hemiramphus balao

A Ballyhoo look-alike, and often called "Ballyhoo," especially in southeastern baitfish markets. Body silver, not greenish as in Ballyhoo. Schools in large numbers near the water's surface, attracting attention of game fish and seabirds, their principal predators. **Range:** New York to Brazil. **Size:** To 9 in. (23 cm).

HALFBEAK
Hyporhamphus unifasciatus

Note long bright orange-red lower jaw. Favorite food of Dolphin, billfish, and mackerel. Large schools feed near the water's surface and are often seen skittering away from approaching boats. **Range:** Maine to Argentina. **Size:** To 10.5 in. (27 cm).

ATLANTIC NEEDLEFISH
Strongylura marina

Active mainly at night, coming readily to night lights on bait boats to hunt small fish, its principal prey. Easily separated from other halfbeaks by brown upperparts and silvery underparts. **Range:** Maine to Brazil. **Size:** To 25 in. (64 cm).

NORTHERN SAND LANCE
Ammodytes dubius

Abundant species, important food resource for seabirds, seals, game fish, whales, and dolphins. Whales such as Humpback and Fin herd schools to the ocean surface, where the water seems to boil with Sand Lance frantic to escape the whales' jaws. **Range:** Labrador to North Carolina. **Size:** To 7 in. (18 cm).

BAITFISH

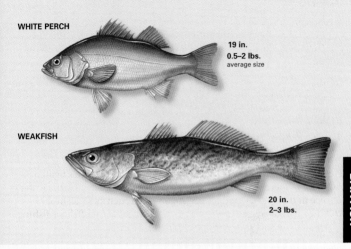

WHITE PERCH

19 in.
0.5–2 lbs.
average size

WEAKFISH

20 in.
2–3 lbs.

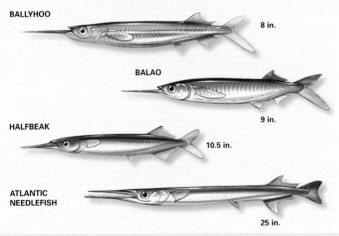

BALLYHOO

8 in.

BALAO

9 in.

HALFBEAK

10.5 in.

ATLANTIC NEEDLEFISH

25 in.

NORTHERN SAND LANCE

7 in.

MACKEREL

WAHOO
Acanthocybium solandri

The largest mackerel. Elongated body, with head tapering into beak-like shape. Distinct creamy vertical stripes wrap around its body. Its tenacity and fight make Wahoo an esteemed game fish. May weigh up to 100 lbs. (45 kg). **Range:** Southern; wanders to Massachusetts. **Size:** To 7 ft. (2.1 m).

KING MACKEREL
Scomberomorus cavalla

Large, voracious. Spectacular royal blue above and silver below. Very swift swimmer. Comes inshore to hunt in bays. Excellent eating, but flesh spoils quickly, causing scombroid food poisoning. **Range:** Southern; wanders to Massachusetts. **Size:** To 5.5 ft. (1.7 m).

CERO
Scomberomorus regalis

Similar to Spanish Mackerel, but with yellow pectoral and anal fins. Side streaked with yellow-brown; spots above and below lateral line. Scales cover body, including pectoral fins. Solitary. **Range:** Southern; wanders to Massachusetts. **Size:** To 3.5 ft. (1 m).

SPANISH MACKEREL
Scomberomorus maculatus

Bluish green to blue, with distinct yellowish brown to gold mid-side spotting. Common game fish that schools near shores feeding on baitfish. Sensitive to water turbidity and pollution. **Range:** Massachusetts to Mexico. **Size:** To 3 ft. (91 cm).

ATLANTIC MACKEREL
Scomber scombrus

Very dark-backed with silver underparts. Occurs in large schools. Back marked with wavy bands; belly whitish. No spotting on sides. Important commercial fish, common inshore during summer. **Range:** Labrador to Cape Hatteras. **Size:** To 22 in. (56 cm).

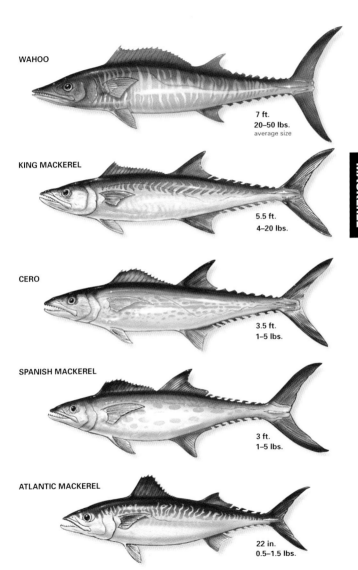

WAHOO

7 ft.
20–50 lbs.
average size

KING MACKEREL

5.5 ft.
4–20 lbs.

CERO

3.5 ft.
1–5 lbs.

SPANISH MACKEREL

3 ft.
1–5 lbs.

ATLANTIC MACKEREL

22 in.
0.5–1.5 lbs.

MACKEREL

SMALLER TUNA

Small to medium tuna species. Most are swift, offshore predators and support large sport and commercial fisheries in the Western Atlantic.

BULLET MACKEREL   *Auxis rochei*

More tuna-shaped than elongate like other mackerel, with beautiful purple tint to back and nearly vertical barring. Unspotted sides distinguish it from near look-alike Frigate Mackerel. **Range:** Bay of Fundy to Florida. **Weight:** To 15 lbs. (7 kg). **Size:** To 20 in. (51 cm).

FRIGATE MACKEREL   *Auxis thazard*

Very similar to Bullet Mackerel but less purple tint and more oblique lines on back. One to five distinct spots below pectoral fin. **Range:** Mainly tropical waters; sometimes wanders north in Gulf Stream to offshore New York. **Weight:** To 15 lbs. (7 kg). **Size:** To 20 in. (51 cm).

LITTLE TUNNY   *Euthynnus alletteratus*

Irregular jigsaw pattern on back, numerous spots on sides and below pectoral fins. Occurs in large schools, perhaps the most common tuna off northeast coast. **Range:** Massachusetts to Brazil. **Weight:** To 25 lbs. (11 kg). **Size:** To 39 in. (1 m).

BLACKFIN TUNA   *Thunnus atlanticus*

Long, thin pectoral fin. Dusky second dorsal fin. All finlets dusky with white edges. Broad yellow-brown stripe on upper body. **Range:** Massachusetts coast to Brazil. **Weight:** To 40 lbs. (18 kg). **Size:** To 39 in. (1 m).

ATLANTIC BONITO   *Sarda sarda*

Bluish above fading to white below with distinct broad greenish stripes on the back. An important commercial fish but cannot be sold as "tuna." **Range:** Migratory. Gulf of St. Lawrence to Argentina, preferring more temperate waters. **Weight:** To 20 lbs. (9 kg). **Size:** To 36 in. (91 cm).

SKIPJACK TUNA   *Euthynnus pelamis*

Easily identified by three to five distinct black stripes on side and belly. Also note slight connection between dorsal fins. Often found in large schools and an important commercial fish. **Range:** Migratory; Nova Scotia and Newfoundland in summer, to Florida and Gulf of Mexico. **Weight:** To 75 lbs. (34 kg). **Size:** To 40 in. (1 m).

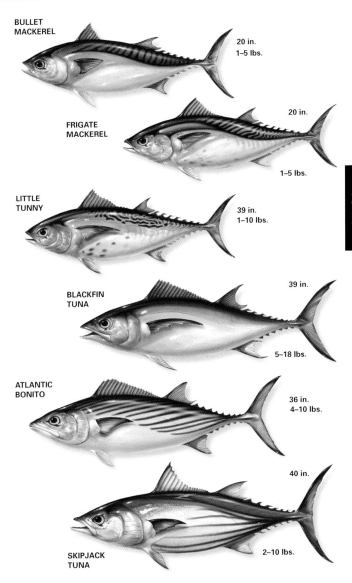

BULLET
MACKEREL

20 in.
1–5 lbs.

FRIGATE
MACKEREL

20 in.

1–5 lbs.

LITTLE
TUNNY

39 in.
1–10 lbs.

BLACKFIN
TUNA

39 in.

5–18 lbs.

ATLANTIC
BONITO

36 in.
4–10 lbs.

SKIPJACK
TUNA

40 in.

2–10 lbs.

TUNA

LARGE TUNA

Large, swift ocean predators, highly prized for their delicious flesh. Most larger tuna species are declining in the western North Atlantic, due to overfishing by commercial fleets.

ALBACORE
Thunnus alalunga

Dark blue backed, silver below. Extremely long pectoral fins. Caudal fin silver with white edge. Finlets yellow. Hunts in large, voracious schools; feeding activity often visible from a distance. **Range:** South Atlantic ranging north regularly to Long Island, rarely to Nova Scotia. **Weight:** To 100 lbs. (45 kg), averaging 20 lbs. (9 kg). **Size:** To 4.5 ft. (1.3 m); most smaller. Red List – Data deficient

YELLOWFIN TUNA
Thunnus albacares

Beautiful deep blue back contrasting to yellow underparts. Second dorsal very long, arched, and rich yellow. Feeds in large schools. **Range:** Nova Scotia to tropics. **Weight:** To over 400 lbs. (181 kg), averaging 20–100 lbs. (9–45 kg). **Size:** To 6 ft. (1.8 m); most smaller in our area.

BIGEYE TUNA
Thunnus obesus

Bluish above, silver below. Note short, blunt head, and very large eye. Finlets yellow with black edges. **Range:** Nova Scotia south; much more common in tropical waters. **Weight:** To 450 lbs. (204 kg). **Size:** To 7.5 ft. (2.3 m), but usually much smaller. Red List – Vulnerable

BLUEFIN TUNA
Thunnus thynnus

Streamlined body, dark back grading to silver on sides, creamy white below. Finlets typically gray to steel blue. Can reach huge size, although typical sizes now much reduced from historic maximums. **Range:** Nova Scotia south. **Weight:** To 500 lbs. (227 kg). **Size:** To 14 ft. (4.3 m), but usually much smaller, averaging 7.5 ft (2.3 m). Red List – Data deficient

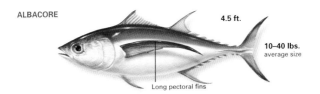

ALBACORE

4.5 ft.

10–40 lbs.
average size

Long pectoral fins

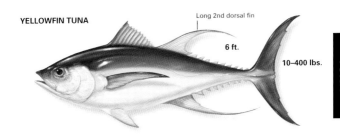

YELLOWFIN TUNA

Long 2nd dorsal fin

6 ft.

10–400 lbs.

TUNA

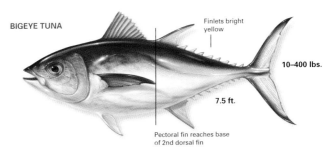

BIGEYE TUNA

Finlets bright
yellow

10–400 lbs.

7.5 ft.

Pectoral fin reaches base
of 2nd dorsal fin

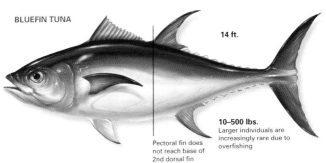

BLUEFIN TUNA

14 ft.

10–500 lbs.
Larger individuals are
increasingly rare due to
overfishing

Pectoral fin does
not reach base of
2nd dorsal fin

BILLFISH

BLUE MARLIN
Makaira nigricans

Massive, with elongate rostrum. Deep blue above fading to white below. Sharp, pointed, low dorsal fin. Complex lateral line, forming net-like pattern on flank. **Range:** Gulf of Maine south; prefers Gulf Stream. **Weight:** Typically 100–300 lbs. (45–136 kg). **Size:** To 15.5 ft. (4.7 m); most smaller.

WHITE MARLIN
Tetrapturus albidus

Large, blue above, white below. Dorsal fin has high, rounded front, higher than depth of body. Anal fin also rounded. Both fins may be spotted. **Range:** Gulf of Maine south in temperate waters. **Weight:** To 180 lbs. (82 kg). **Size:** To 10 ft. (3 m).

LONGBILL SPEARFISH
Tetrapturus pfluegeri

The smallest billfish. Similar to Sailfish, but with smaller, rounded, unspotted sail. No "forehead" hump before dorsal fin, as in Sailfish. **Range:** New Jersey south. **Weight:** To 90 lbs. (41 kg). **Size:** To 6 ft. (1.8 m).

SAILFISH
Istiophorus platypterus

Blue above, white below. Dorsal fin high, sail-like, heavily spotted. Hump on "forehead" before dorsal fin. Very small pectoral fins. Pelvic fins thin and elongate. **Range:** Tropical waters; north in Gulf Stream to New York. **Weight:** To 180 lbs. (82 kg). **Size:** To 11 ft. (3.4 m).

SWORDFISH
Xiphias gladius

The largest billfish. Grayish, greenish, or blue with dark fins. Very long rostrum ("sword"). Long peduncled keel forward and on side of caudal fins. Frequents the water's surface, where it is often harpooned. **Range:** Grand Banks to tropics. **Weight:** To 1,300 lbs. (590 kg). **Size:** To 15 ft. (4.6 m). Red List – Data deficient

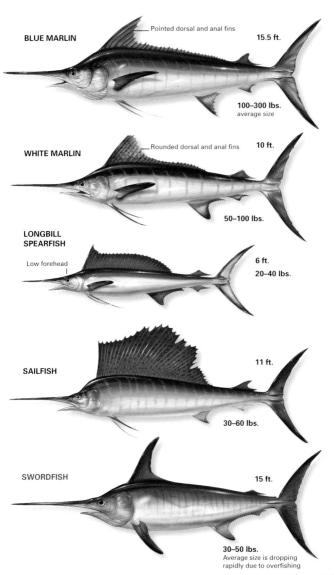

BLUE MARLIN — Pointed dorsal and anal fins — 15.5 ft.

100–300 lbs. average size

WHITE MARLIN — Rounded dorsal and anal fins — 10 ft.

50–100 lbs.

LONGBILL SPEARFISH

Low forehead

6 ft.
20–40 lbs.

SAILFISH

11 ft.

30–60 lbs.

SWORDFISH

15 ft.

30–50 lbs.
Average size is dropping rapidly due to overfishing

BILLFISH

SCULPINS AND SEAROBIN

Sculpins and searobins are bizarre-looking bottom dwellers that occasionally drift to the water's surface. Although capable of short bursts of speed, they spend most of their time "walking" over the seafloor on modified pectoral-fin rays. They are commonly caught accidentally by sportfishers during bottom fishing.

LONGHORN SCULPIN
Myoxocephalus octodecemspinosus

Common bottom feeder found in shallow inshore waters in summer, but moving to deeper offshore waters in winter. Eight or nine very sharp spines on dorsal fin – beware when removing sculpins from a hook. Voracious, diet ranging from fish offal discarded from boats or in dock areas to crabs, fish, and shrimp. **Range:** Cold waters off Newfoundland to Virginia. **Size:** To 18 in. (46 cm).

SHORTHORN SCULPIN
Myoxocephalus scorpius

A cold water sculpin. Mainly found inshore, especially in summer. Sculpins eat a wide variety of food, from crabs, shrimp, and small fish to scraps either tossed overboard or resulting from feeding frenzies of species such as tuna. The Shorthorn Sculpin has been studied for "antifreeze" proteins in its blood that resist freezing in winter. **Range:** Arctic and Canadian Maritime waters, occasionally to New York. **Size:** To 24 in. (61 cm).

SEA RAVEN
Hemitripterus americanus

When taken on hook, often inflates its belly like a puffer. When removing from hook, beware of the long, stiff spines of front portion of dorsal fin. Omnivorous, capturing and eating almost anything it encounters on seafloor. Common in northern range and dwindling in numbers to south. **Range:** North of Cape Cod Bay to Chesapeake Bay. **Size:** To 25 in. (63 cm).

NORTHERN SEAROBIN
Prionotus carolinus

The most common searobin. Bony plates and spines cover head. Uses three long rays of pectoral fins to "walk" on seafloor. Searobins have been taken in waters to a depth of nearly 100 fathoms (183 m). Omnivorous, eating small fish, shrimp, clams, sea worms, and small crabs. Although its meat is edible and quite tasty, its unusual appearance usually guarantees that it is tossed overboard when caught. **Range:** Bay of Fundy to South Carolina. **Size:** To 16 in. (41 cm); most 12 in. (30 cm) or less.

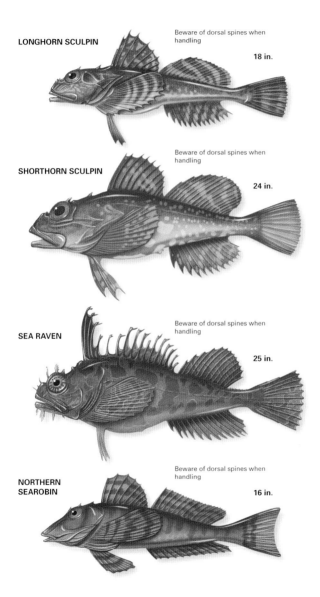

LONGHORN SCULPIN

Beware of dorsal spines when handling

18 in.

SHORTHORN SCULPIN

Beware of dorsal spines when handling

24 in.

SEA RAVEN

Beware of dorsal spines when handling

25 in.

NORTHERN SEAROBIN

Beware of dorsal spines when handling

16 in.

SCULPINS

FLOUNDERS, HALIBUT, GOOSEFISH

Flounders start life like other typical fish, but then they gradually begin to roll to one side, and their eyes migrate to one side of the body. Flounders are classified by which eye becomes dominant and hence designates the upper, pigmented side. There are left-eyed flounders and right-eyed flounders. Goosefish (Lophiidae) are also bottom feeders, flat in shape but not related to flounders.

SUMMER FLOUNDER   *Paralichthys dentatus*

Popular mainstay of commercial fishing industry as well as sportfishing boats and pier fishers. Ranges from gray to brown to nearly black. Prefers inshore sandy bottom areas, moving farther offshore to deeper waters in winter. Although large specimens have reached 3 ft. (91 cm) and 25 lbs. (11 kg), much smaller fish ranging 2–5 lbs. (1–2 kg) are now usual. **Range:** Maine to South Carolina in continental waters. **Size:** To 3 ft. (91 cm), but typically much smaller.

WINTER FLOUNDER (LEMON SOLE) *Pseudopleuronectes americanus*

Also known as "flatfish," this species is well known to sportfishers. Mainly a shallow-water species that ranges from Labrador to Chesapeake Bay. Larger individuals are found in deeper water in excess of 350 fathoms. Winter Flounders migrate from deep offshore waters to shallow coastal waters in the fall, and move back to deep waters in the spring. Larger individuals can be nearly 2 ft. (61 cm) long and weigh up to 5 lbs. (2 kg). Winter Flounders caught off Rhode Island are often quite large, and locals refer to them as "snowshoes." **Range:** Labrador to Chesapeake Bay. **Size:** Typically 15 in. (38 cm), to 24 in. (61 cm).

ATLANTIC HALIBUT   *Hippoglossus hippoglossus*

Former mainstay of east coast fishing industry, now overfished throughout range. Large, bottom-feeding flounder that eats other fish, including cod, herring, and skates. Halibut in turn is food for seals and is taken by Greenland Sharks in northern waters. **Range:** Greenland to New Jersey coast in cooler waters. **Size:** Formerly to 6 ft. (1.8 m) or more, now typically 3–4 ft. (91 cm–1.2 m) or less. Red List – Endangered

GOOSEFISH   *Lophius americanus*

One of the ugliest fishes. Relative of deep-sea Anglerfish, as shown by its highly modified dorsal fin, which arises from the upper lip and acts as a fishing lure for small prey fish. Typically found in shallow water in cold months, migrating to deeper waters in summer. **Range:** Newfoundland to North Carolina. **Size:** To 4 ft. (1.2 m).

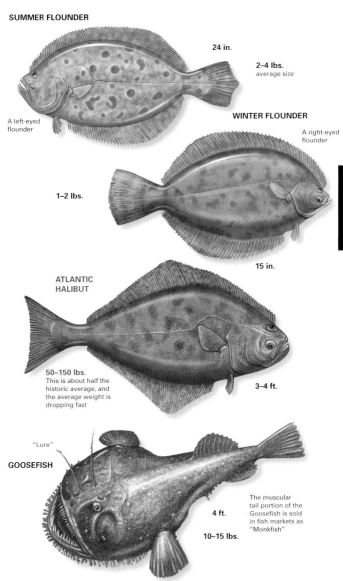

SUMMER FLOUNDER

24 in.

2–4 lbs.
average size

A left-eyed
flounder

WINTER FLOUNDER

A right-eyed
flounder

1–2 lbs.

15 in.

FLOUNDERS

**ATLANTIC
HALIBUT**

50–150 lbs.
This is about half the
historic average, and
the average weight is
dropping fast

3–4 ft.

"Lure"

GOOSEFISH

4 ft.

10–15 lbs.

The muscular
tail portion of the
Goosefish is sold
in fish markets as
"Monkfish"

OCEAN SUNFISH   *Masturus lanceolatus, Mola mola*

These pelagic giants are unmistakable – massive with a flattened circular body that looks as if it had been cut off in the rear. The mouth is small, and the gill opening has been reduced to a mere hole. Molas lack pectoral fins, and the dorsal and anal fins have exceptionally long rays, giving them a sailboat-like appearance from the side. When seen floating near the water's surface they are often accompanied by seabirds picking at parasites found in the thick mucus covering of the skin. It is believed that many of these surface floaters are either sick individuals or are stunned by cold water. Rarely they may be found drifting in close to the shoreline. These large fish are much more sluggish in the cold waters of the north that lie outside the Gulf Stream current and are easily captured in such a languid state. They feed mainly on oceanic jellyfish like the Portuguese Man-Of-War, other invertebrates, and some larval fish. These species are worldwide in distribution in tropical waters.

SHARPTAIL MOLA   *Masturus lanceolatus*

A massive fish, very similar to Ocean Sunfish. Caudal "fin" shows distinct central projection, hence name "sharptail." Often seen floating listlessly at the water's surface with dorsal projecting into air. This behavior is not typical of healthy adults, and Molas who surface may be injured or dying. Though very large, harmless unless attacked. Not considered edible. **Weight:** To 2 tons (1.8 t) or more. **Size:** To 10 ft. (3 m) long and 11 ft. (3.3 m) high.

OCEAN SUNFISH   *Mola mola*

Massive disc-like body, brownish olive to brownish gray. Mouth tiny and round. Elongate vertical rays in tall dorsal and anal fins are used to scull water in tropical areas, where sunfish can swim remarkably fast. Dorsal fin often projects from the water's surface. Caudal "fin" is merely a wavy flap of uniform width, with no projection as in Sharptail Mola. **Weight:** To 2 tons (1.8 t) or more. **Size:** To 10 ft. (3 m) long and 11 ft. (3.3 m) high.

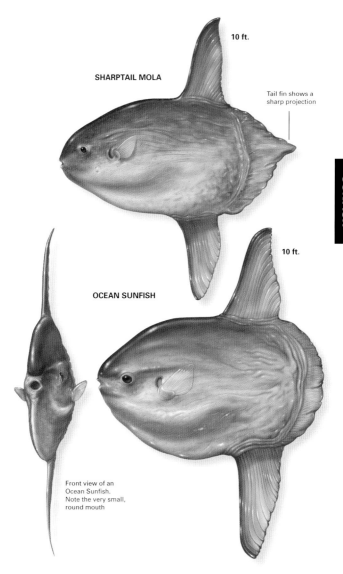

10 ft.

SHARPTAIL MOLA

Tail fin shows a
sharp projection

OCEAN SUNFISH

10 ft.

SUNFISH

Front view of an
Ocean Sunfish.
Note the very small,
round mouth

65

GREEN AND HAWKSBILL TURTLES

Sea turtles are mainly inhabitants of tropical waters. Occasionally turtles wander into very cold northern waters and are numbed. The cold-shocked turtles wash ashore or may helplessly wallow at the water's surface. The smaller turtle species are sometimes difficult to identify when seen at the surface. They are often covered with barnacles and may be in poor physical condition with battered shells. In some cases only a careful examination of the scutes (bony plates) of the shell will confirm an identification. Beware of handling these large, powerful animals. Even hypothermic turtles can bite or strike out with their flippers. Sea turtles are protected animals in all U.S. waters and should not be handled unless they are fouled in fishing gear, and then only with great caution. Contact a marine animal rescue unit rather than attempting to save a turtle yourself.

GREEN SEA TURTLE
Chelonia mydas

Olive-brown overall. Shell flecked and mottled with lighter patterns. Large head distinctly scaled, with pale margins on scales. Front flippers exceptionally large. At times swims at the water's surface with a bobbing motion, its back alternately surfacing and dipping below water. Feeds principally on sea grass, crabs, jellyfish, and invertebrates. The only U.S. nesting area is in Florida. **Range:** Cape Cod south; uncommon north of New Jersey. **Size:** To 5 ft. (1.5 m).

ATLANTIC HAWKSBILL
Eretmochelys imbricata

Rich chestnut-brown shell with black and yellow radiation marks. Distinct ridge runs down center of carapace, forming central keel on back. Upper jaw elongated into namesake "hawk's bill." Feeds principally on jellyfish, crabs, sponges, and marine algae. Nests on Caribbean beaches. Most common in tropical waters, especially near coral reefs. Drifts northward in Gulf Stream. Atlantic Hawksbill numbers have suffered greatly due to hunting for shells and meat. **Range:** Cape Cod south. **Size:** To 3 ft. (91 cm). **Red List – Critically endangered**

GREEN SEA TURTLE

5 ft.

ATLANTIC HAWKSBILL

3 ft.

LOGGERHEAD AND RIDLEY TURTLES

LOGGERHEAD SEA TURTLE
Caretta caretta

Bright reddish brown shell is diagnostic, as is sharp, squared-off jawline. Shell elongated, with serrated ridges on rear edges. Large head with distinctive hump at nape. The most inshore of the marine turtles, regularly entering bays and estuaries. Diet includes mollusks, sponges, invertebrates, turtle grass, and marine algae. Nests along east coast between April and August. Regularly nests as far north as Carolinas, rarely into Maryland. Loggerheads can live up to 20 years. **Range:** Commonly wanders north to Nova Scotia; casual north to Newfoundland. **Size:** To 7 ft. (2.1 m). **Red List – Endangered**

ATLANTIC RIDLEY
Lepidochelys kempi

Small size and prominent back ridges are diagnostic. Olive-green to yellowish in color; pale individuals can be nearly white. Swims high in water, affording good view of double-back keel and allowing identification. Shell heart-shaped with three ridges. Lateral back ridges become less prominent with age. Overall shape more rounded and compact than other sea turtles. Diet includes crabs, mollusks, and fish. Nests mainly in Texas and Mexico, rarely in Florida. **Range:** Uncommon north of Cape Hatteras, north to Cape Cod; young wanderers straggle to Nova Scotia. **Size:** To 29 in. (74 cm). **Red List – Critically endangered**

LOGGERHEAD SEA TURTLE

7 ft.

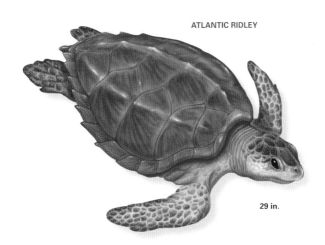

ATLANTIC RIDLEY

29 in.

LEATHERBACK SEA TURTLE

Dermochelys coriacea

Distinctive features: The largest sea turtle. Bluish black to dark gray, flecked with white or pinkish spotting in scattered locations. Seven prominent ridges arise from flexible carapace. Note very long front flippers. **Red List – Critically endangered**

Description and size: This huge turtle can reach 9 ft. (2.7 m) in length and weigh more than 1,500 lbs. (680 kg), with record animals weighing in at over a ton. When viewed from above, the leathery-skinned "shell" tapers toward the rear, giving the Leatherback a heart-shaped appearance.

Habits: A wanderer of the deep oceans, this animal is remarkably adapted to range into the cold North Atlantic waters. Late in the season these waters at times become too cold, and numbed individuals float ashore and can be found beached. The Leatherback's diet consists mainly of jellyfish, making this turtle one of the few animals to use this group as a food source. When it encounters large masses of jellyfish, it can spend hours feeding in the area. Normally solitary. Groups can be encountered on occasion, especially during concentrated jellyfish outbreaks.

Similar species: When well viewed, the flexible carapace with its prominent ridges and the animal's overall size make this species unmistakable.

Prominent ridges along shell

Shell tapers to a point

9 ft.

TURTLES

LOONS AND GREBES

Loons and grebes are long-necked diving birds most commonly seen in marine waters during spring and fall migration and when wintering in salt water. These birds rarely venture far offshore.

COMMON LOON
Gavia immer

A large, heavy-bodied bird mainly of inshore waters. Long, heavy bill is adapted to capture fish during deep dives. Seen mainly in winter and during spring and fall migration. Winter bird is dark-backed and white below. Bill held parallel to water and not uptilted. **Length:** 30 in. (76 cm). **Wingspan:** 58 in. (147 cm).

RED-THROATED LOON
Gavia stellata

Distinguished from Common Loon by smaller size and thin, upturned bill. In winter plumage, much grayer than Common Loon. Thin bill usually points upward. Favors inshore waters. Seen mainly in winter and during spring and fall migration. **Length:** 25 in. (64 cm). **Wingspan:** 44 in. (112 cm).

RED-NECKED GREBE
Podiceps grisegena

A medium-sized diving bird, one of the larger grebes. In winter plumage, dark gray back with light gray underparts. Head capped with black, contrasting with nearly white cheeks and throat. Long, sharp bill, but much more delicate than loon's. **Length:** 19 in. (48 cm). **Wingspan:** 33 in. (84 cm).

HORNED GREBE
Podiceps auritus

A very small diving bird with dark gray back and light gray to white underparts. Top of head appears black-capped. Light gray throat and cheeks. Delicate, short bill. Not a deep ocean bird, favoring inshore waters. Often seen in flocks of hundreds at harbor mouths. **Length:** 13 in. (33 cm). **Wingspan:** 25 in. (64 cm).

COMMON LOON

Winter

Head is
held lower
than body

Winter

Long,
heavy bill

Winter

Upturned bill

Winter

**RED-THROATED
LOON**

Winter

**RED-NECKED
GREBE**

Winter

Winter

**HORNED
GREBE**

Winter

Winter

ALBATROSSES, FRIGATEBIRD, TROPICBIRD

The following four species of seabirds are very easy to identify based on their size or dramatic color. The albatrosses are extremely rare, whereas the Tropicbird and the Frigatebird are seen with more consistency, especially in the Gulf Stream area off Cape Hatteras.

YELLOW-NOSED ALBATROSS — *Diomedea chlororhynchos*

Black back contrasts with white underparts. White underwings. Bill diagnostic: black with yellow line running down crest. An oceanic wanderer. Often follows boats and comes in to hang in the wind off the stern. Attracted to groups of feeding pelagic birds. **Length:** 32 in. (81 cm). **Wingspan:** 80 in. (2 m).

BLACK-BROWED ALBATROSS — *Diomedea melanophris*

Dark back and white underparts. Leading edge of underwing extensively black. Entire wing has sooty cast compared to white underwings of the Yellow-nosed. Bright yellow bill, gray in immature birds. Black smear runs below brow of eye. **Length:** 35 in. (89 cm). **Wingspan:** 88 in. (2.2 m).

MAGNIFICENT FRIGATEBIRD — *Fregata magnificens*

Long-winged but streamlined. Note long, forked tail. Male solid black, throat pouch usually hidden from view. Female has white underbelly. Immature has all-white head and white underbelly. Pursues and robs food from other seabirds. **Length:** 40 in. (102 cm). **Wingspan:** 92 in. (2.3 m).

WHITE-TAILED TROPICBIRD — *Phaethon lepturus*

Unmistakable. Beautiful white seabird with bold black chevrons on back and very long white tail streaming behind. Yellow bill. Immature has black-barred back. Buoyant flight. Inquisitive; will join other seabirds in feeding flocks. **Length:** 31 in. (79 cm). **Wingspan:** 38 in. (97 cm).

ALBATROSSES, FRIGATEBIRD, TROPICBIRD

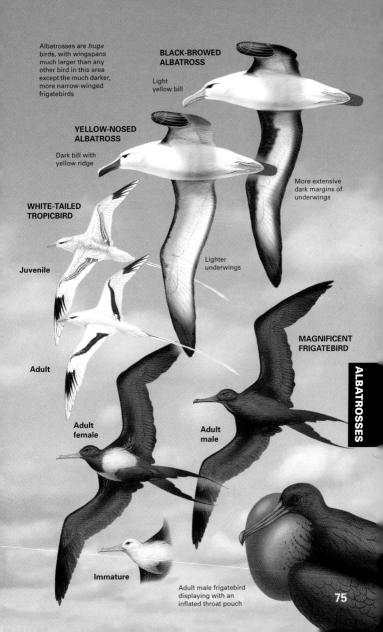

Albatrosses are *huge* birds, with wingspans much larger than any other bird in this area except the much darker, more narrow-winged frigatebirds

BLACK-BROWED ALBATROSS

Light yellow bill

YELLOW-NOSED ALBATROSS

Dark bill with yellow ridge

More extensive dark margins of underwings

WHITE-TAILED TROPICBIRD

Juvenile

Lighter underwings

Adult

MAGNIFICENT FRIGATEBIRD

Adult female

Adult male

Immature

Adult male frigatebird displaying with an inflated throat pouch

ALBATROSSES

75

LARGE SHEARWATERS

Shearwaters have long, thin wings that are perfectly adapted for high speed over the ocean surface. Their wingtips occasionally slice into the waves of turbulent water, hence the name "shearwater." The stiff, unflexed wingbeat of shearwaters separates them from all other seabirds. Shearwaters nest in the South Atlantic during the austral summer and spend the austral winter (our summer) in North Atlantic waters.

GREATER SHEARWATER   *Puffinus gravis*

A large shearwater with distinctive black cap delineated by white nape. Hard separation between dark upper parts and white underbelly. Stark white rump contrasts with dark back. Note dark underbelly smudge. The most common shearwater in our offshore waters; hundreds can be seen at times. Comes readily to chum. **Length:** 18 in. (46 cm). **Wingspan:** 44 in. (112 cm).

CORY'S SHEARWATER   *Calonectris diomedea*

The largest of our shearwaters. Underbelly lacks dark smudge of Greater Shearwater. Note distinct yellow bill. Flight sequence is usually four slow flaps followed by a long glide. Never common or even regular in our area, usually seen individually. Comes quite close to land and can be seen from ferries to islands such as Nantucket. **Length:** 20 in. (51 cm). **Wingspan:** 44 in. (112 cm).

SOOTY SHEARWATER   *Puffinus griseus*

Appears as all brown, but note gray-white underwings. One of the most common shearwaters. At times hundreds mass on the ocean surface, apparently feeding on floating krill. Readily approaches ships and will come to chumming and settle on the water. **Length:** 17 in. (43 cm). **Wingspan:** 43 in. (109 cm).

GREATER
SHEARWATER

Black
cap and
smudge
on belly

CORY'S
SHEARWATER

Cap is
smudgy
and
lacks
contrast

SOOTY
SHEARWATER

BLACK-CAPPED
PETREL

Off the Carolina
coast, the large Black-
capped Petrel may
be confused with the
Greater Shearwater;
the petrel has a white
forehead and a much
broader rump patch

Gray
wing
linings

SHEARWATERS

NORTHERN FULMAR

Fulmarus glacialis

Description and size: This medium-sized seabird is superficially similar to a gull. The body proportions, however, are quite different: Fulmars are much bulkier and thicker-necked than gulls, and they have a high, domed forehead. The Northern Fulmar has two distinct color phases. Most Fulmars in our area are light-phase birds, but dark-phase individuals also occur regularly. Intermediate-phase birds blend the characteristics of the dark and light phases. **Length:** 19 in. (48 cm). **Wingspan:** 43 in. (109 cm).

Habits: Although they look much like gulls, Fulmars behave very differently, and this makes them fairly easy to distinguish from gulls. Fulmars have a distinctive, stiff-winged glide that is closer to the flight of shearwaters than it is to any gull flight pattern. Fulmars are deep-ocean wanderers that readily follow ships and take chum. They are often seen near feeding whales, looking for scraps and injured fish. The population has increased dramatically in the past two decades.

Similar species: At longer ranges, light-phase Fulmars are first distinguished from gulls by their stiff-winged flight characteristics and chunkier body silhouette. Unlike gulls, Fulmars are rarely seen within sight of land, except near their arctic nesting colonies. Dark-phase Fulmars are similar in color to Sooty Shearwaters but have much bulkier bodies and proportionately broader wings than the slimmer, more slender-winged shearwaters.

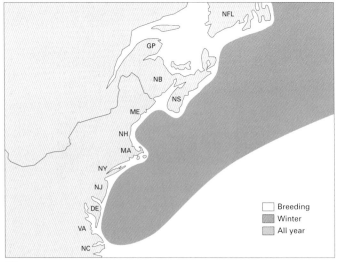

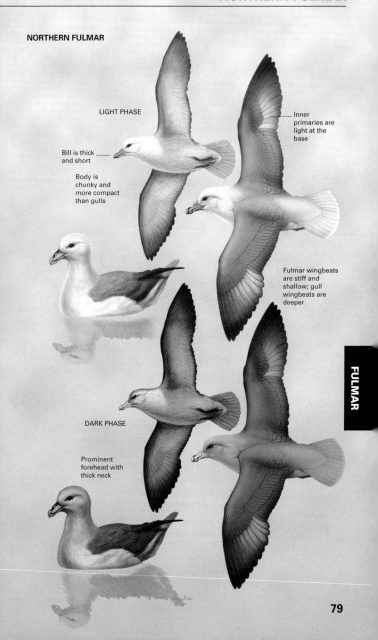

NORTHERN FULMAR

LIGHT PHASE

Bill is thick and short

Body is chunky and more compact than gulls

Inner primaries are light at the base

Fulmar wingbeats are stiff and shallow; gull wingbeats are deeper

DARK PHASE

Prominent forehead with thick neck

FULMAR

SMALL SHEARWATERS

Three species of small, closely related shearwaters. Only the Manx Shearwater is commonly seen. Audubon's Shearwater is more frequent south of Virginia; the Little Shearwater is very rare.

AUDUBON'S SHEARWATER   *Puffinus lherminieri*

The smallest of our regularly occurring shearwaters. Near look-alike to Manx Shearwater but with dark undertail and distinctly longer tail. Best clue is flight pattern, very fluttery and fast as the bird rocks back and forth over the water. Single birds are usually seen and, because of their small size, can be overlooked when mixing with larger shearwater species. **Length:** 12 in. (31 cm). **Wingspan:** 27 in. (69 cm).

LITTLE SHEARWATER   *Puffinus assimilis*

A very rare summer visitor to southern and mid-Atlantic coastal and offshore waters. One of the smallest shearwaters. Darker above than Audubon's Shearwater and with more white on face than Manx Shearwater. Closely related to Audubon's Shearwater and classed by some authors as a race of Audubon's rather than as a separate species. **Length:** 11 in. (28 cm). **Wingspan:** 25 in. (64 cm).

MANX SHEARWATER   *Puffinus puffinus*

A small black-and-white shearwater, half the size of bulky Greater Shearwater. Lacks Greater's capped appearance and white rump. Flight is very buoyant and bounding, as if being pulled up by a string while fluttering on stiff wings. Look for white under the tail. Favors inshore waters, often appearing within sight of land. Numbers appear to be increasing in the past two decades. **Length:** 14 in. (36 cm). **Wingspan:** 33 in. (84 cm).

AUDUBON'S SHEARWATER

LITTLE SHEARWATER

Dark leading edge of wing lining

More white on face

Back is almost black

Long tail

Light leading edge of wing lining

White under tail

MANX SHEARWATER

RARE PELAGICS

Look for but do not expect to see the following species. Exploration of the Gulf Stream off the Carolina coast has revealed an area rich with spectacular finds. These warm waters act as a pathway for species that wander north from the tropics. The intersection of the Gulf Stream with the cold Labrador current sweeping down from the north produces unique upwellings and turbulence that attract many rare pelagics.

BLACK-CAPPED PETREL
Pterodroma hasitata

Very large, like a shearwater. Dark gray with white forehead and distinct U-shaped white rump patch. White wing linings. Note distinct bend to wing and fluttery flight pattern. Rollercoaster-like flight, soaring up well above water, then plunging down with bowed wings. Breeds on Caribbean islands. **Length:** 16 in. (41 cm). **Wingspan:** 37 in. (94 cm).

HERALD (TRINIDAD) PETREL
Pterodroma arminjoniana

Also called Harcourt's Petrel. A large gadfly petrel. Three distinct color phases with intermediate types. All phases have tail tapered to a point and large white patches at base of outer underwing feathers. Leading underwing edge also white. Rapid wing beats, rollercoaster-like flight, speeding upward well above the water before plunging downward on bent-back wings. **Length:** 15 in. (38 cm). **Wingspan:** 35 in. (89 cm). Red List – Vulnerable

SOFT-PLUMAGED (FEA'S) PETREL
Pterodroma feae

Dark eye line, barred forehead, white belly, and incomplete dark collar band. Like other *Pterodroma*s, this petrel is a fast flyer that scales in over the water on stiff wingbeats, then shoots upward well above the surface and glides back down. Holds wings in bent position. Breeds in late May and early June off the Carolina coast. **Length:** 15 in. (38 cm). **Wingspan:** 34 in. (86 cm). Red List – Near threatened

GREATER SHEARWATER

Shown for comparison

A much larger bird with broader, more rounded wings

BLACK-CAPPED PETREL

White collar

White upper tail

White breast and belly

Dark bar on underside of wings

HERALD PETREL

Uniformly dark above and below

SOFT-PLUMAGED PETREL

Gray nape

Heralds seen off the east coast are the darkest form, showing little or no white on the body

RARITIES

STORM-PETRELS

These "storm" birds are drawn to severe storms at sea, where they feed in the roiled waters. The name "petrel" derives from the biblical story of Saint Peter walking on the water; when these small birds feed on plankton, they often dangle their feet, giving the appearance of walking on water.

WILSON'S STORM-PETREL
Oceanites oceanicus

Small and black with a white rump patch. Has the skimming flight of a swallow. Patters about on water's surface when feeding. If viewing up close, try to note square end of tail. At close range, feet can be seen extending beyond tail tip. Yellow toe webbing.

Perhaps the world's most common bird. Roams the high seas worldwide, feeding on planktonic life. Can be chummed near boats by tossing out fish oil and puffed rice. Breeds in burrows along Antarctic coast. Common in North Atlantic waters in summer. **Length:** 7.5 in. (19 cm). **Wingspan:** 16 in. (41 cm).

LEACH'S STORM-PETREL
Oceanodroma leucorhoa

Very similar to Wilson's Storm-Petrel, but note forked tail. Dark chocolate brown with grayish shoulders. Black toe webbing. Unique bouncing, veering flight pattern; from a distance, Leach's Storm-Petrels suggest black butterflies fluttering erratically at the water surface. Uncommon.

Breeds along North Atlantic coast in burrows dug into dirt banks and in rock crevices along shorelines and offshore islands. Leaves and returns to burrow under cover of night. Feeds far out to sea. Winters south of breeding areas, with scattered records of lone birds seen at sea as far north as New Jersey. **Length:** 7.5 in. (19 cm). **Wingspan:** 19 in. (48 cm).

White
upper
tail

WILSON'S
STORM-PETREL

Rounded or
squared tail

LEACH'S
STORM-PETREL

Dark line
divides
white rump
patch

Notched
tail
feathers

Pale upper
wing
coverts

White barely
visible on
rump or sides

RARE STORM-PETRELS

Two rare species of storm-petrel very similar in shape to the common Wilson's and Leach's Storm-Petrels described on the preceding pages. Look for these unusual petrels mixed in with masses of the more common petrels, Northern Fulmars, and shearwaters.

WHITE-FACED STORM-PETREL   *Pelagodroma marina*

A rare, deep ocean petrel. Grayish with white underparts, gray rump, and white face with strong white eye line. Flies low to water with feet dangling, bouncing up and down like a puppet on a string. While feeding often swings side to side like a pendulum. Mainly a bird of southern oceans. Occurs in our area principally from late July through September, far offshore, mixed with other petrels at upwellings along the continental shelf. **Length:** 7.5 in. (19 cm). **Wingspan:** 18 in. (46 cm).

BAND-RUMPED STORM-PETREL   *Oceanodroma castro*

Very similar in appearance to Wilson's Storm-Petrel but larger and generally darker. Area of white on rump is more extensive. Often overlooked because it mixes in with masses of Wilson's. Flight is shearwater-like, with deep wingbeats followed by long glides on stiff wings. Search any large gatherings of petrels far offshore for this uncommon species. Known to occur as far north as the Grand Banks, where it is rare or casual, and in the Gulf Stream of the southern Atlantic coast. **Length:** 9 in. (23 cm). **Wingspan:** 20 in. (51 cm).

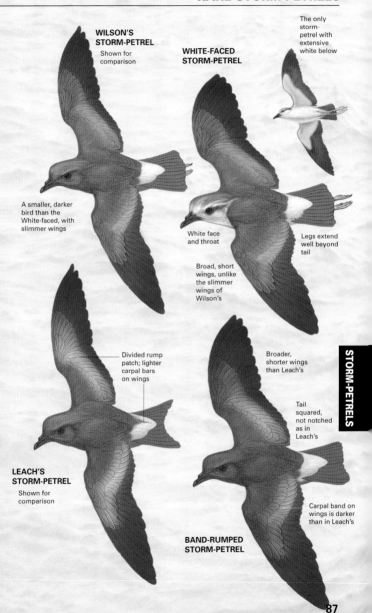

WILSON'S STORM-PETREL
Shown for comparison

WHITE-FACED STORM-PETREL

The only storm-petrel with extensive white below

A smaller, darker bird than the White-faced, with slimmer wings

White face and throat

Legs extend well beyond tail

Broad, short wings, unlike the slimmer wings of Wilson's

Divided rump patch; lighter carpal bars on wings

Broader, shorter wings than Leach's

Tail squared, not notched as in Leach's

LEACH'S STORM-PETREL
Shown for comparison

Carpal band on wings is darker than in Leach's

BAND-RUMPED STORM-PETREL

STORM-PETRELS

BROWN PELICAN

Pelecanus occidentalis

Description and size: This familiar species is one of our largest birds, larger even than the Northern Gannet. The pouched bill is unique to pelicans. Adult is brownish gray with fine gray feathering. Rich chestnut hind neck, yellow crown and throat. Juvenile is mottled brown on back and light brown on breast and belly. Immature bird has a mix of juvenile and adult characteristics; three years are required to develop full adult plumage. **Length:** 48 in. (1.2 m). **Wingspan:** 90 in. (2.3 m).

Habits: Found around marinas perched on posts, boats, and docks as well as on breakwaters and offshore rocks. Often seen plunge-diving for food or skimming water in undulating lines of birds following wave troughs. At long distances the splashes from these dives are a good field mark for feeding pelicans. Pelicans will follow boats (especially fishing boats) a moderate distance offshore looking for food, but they are not true oceanic birds. Brown Pelicans are very common on the east and west coasts of Florida and are common along the southern Atlantic seaboard north to North Carolina. The population of Brown Pelicans has been expanding northward, and the birds are now seen regularly as far north as New Jersey.

Similar species: Unique. If you can't recognize a Brown Pelican, hang up your binoculars.

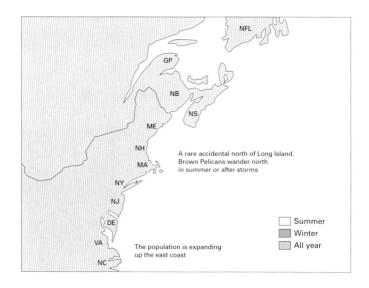

A rare accidental north of Long Island. Brown Pelicans wander north in summer or after storms

☐ Summer
▨ Winter
▨ All year

The population is expanding up the east coast

BROWN PELICAN

Breeding adult
(summer plumage)

BROWN PELICAN

Juvenile
(first-year bird)

Nonbreeding adult
(winter plumage)

Breeding adult
(summer plumage)

PELICAN

89

NORTHERN GANNET

Morus bassanus

Description and size: Adult is very large and white with black outer wings. Juvenile is variable brown; young birds gradually become lighter over several years toward adulthood. The largest indigenous seabird in the Northwest Atlantic. Note white pointed tail and very large bill, giving the body a "double-pointed" look. At close ranges, the golden tint over the adult bird's head and nape may be visible. **Length:** 37 in. (94 cm). **Wingspan:** 72 in. (1.8 m).

Habits: Gannets breed in large colonies on seaward cliffs around the mouth of the Gulf of St. Lawrence, such as Bonaventure Island, Quebec, and at numerous sites along the eastern Newfoundland coast. In winter they range widely at sea, wandering south as winter approaches. When feeding they make spectacular dives into the sea from heights of 40 ft. (12 m) or more. At long distances the splashes from these dives are a good field mark for Gannets. Gregarious, they are often seen in the company of other seabirds over shoals of smaller schooling fish. They sometimes roost on the water in loose rafts of a few dozen individuals. In winter Gannets range from about one mile offshore out to the edge of the continental shelf. However, they are often seen from shore on Cape Cod, Cape Ann, and other coastal headlands when strong onshore winds bring them near land.

Similar species: Much larger than any gull. No gull has a long, pointed tail, and gulls never plunge headlong into the water.

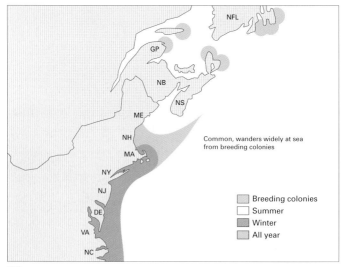

NFL

GP

NB

NS

ME

NH

Common, wanders widely at sea
from breeding colonies

MA

NY

NJ

DE

VA

NC

- Breeding colonies
- Summer
- Winter
- All year

First-year
juvenile

Second- or
third-year
immature

Adult plumage
(at least five
years old)

Outer wings are
black to the wrist,
unlike the more
limited black
wingtips of gulls

NORTHERN
GANNET

Adult
plumage

The heavy bill,
shielded nostrils, and
thick head plumage
are adaptations to
diving from great
heights into the sea

First-year
immature

GANNET

BOOBIES

MASKED BOOBY
BROWN BOOBY

Sula dactylatra
Sula leucogaster

Relatives of the Northern Gannet, these two species are tropical birds that occasionally stray north on the Gulf Stream as far as the North Carolina coast. The Masked Booby looks like a Northern Gannet, but with black secondaries, black tail, and black face mask. The Brown's dark brown neck contrasts with the white belly. Immatures of both species are similar (see plate at right). The Masked Booby feeds on flyingfish, the Brown on a variety of fish. **Length:** 16 in. (41 cm). **Wingspan:** 37 in. (94 cm).

BROWN BOOBY

Adult

Juvenile
(first-year bird)

MASKED BOOBY

Adult

Juvenile
(first-year bird)

MASKED BOOBY

Adult

Black secondaries

Black tail

Juvenile
(first-year bird)

NORTHERN GANNET
Shown for comparison

Gannets are larger than boobies and are rarely seen south of Cape Cod in summer

White tail

White secondaries

BROWN BOOBY

Juvenile
(first-year bird)

Adult

Brown Boobies are uniformly dark above

BOOBIES

93

CORMORANTS

Cormorants are large, dark waterbirds that are increasingly common along the Atlantic coast. Not truly oceanic, these birds are familiar inhabitants of most harbors from Canada to Florida. Unlike other marine birds, cormorants dry their wings by standing with wings outstretched. In flight cormorants look like geese, but their dark coloration and "uphill" angle of the body in flight differ from geese and Brant.

GREAT CORMORANT   *Phalacrocorax carbo*

Bulkier body and proportionately shorter and thicker neck than more common Double-crested Cormorant. In summer, flanks show large white patches. Immature and some winter birds have white belly and dark throat and neck. This is a northern cormorant. In winter, the Great becomes the wintering cormorant in New England, since most Double-crested Cormorants move south of New York. **Length:** 36 in. (91 cm). **Wingspan:** 63 in. (1.6 m).

DOUBLE-CRESTED CORMORANT   *Phalacrocorax auritus*

The common summer cormorant of Atlantic coast. Usually encountered sitting on breakwaters outside harbors. Erect stance, long, angular neck, and uptilted bill are all characteristic. An inshore species that rarely ventures out of sight of land. **Length:** 32 in. (81 cm). **Wingspan:** 52 in. (1.3 m).

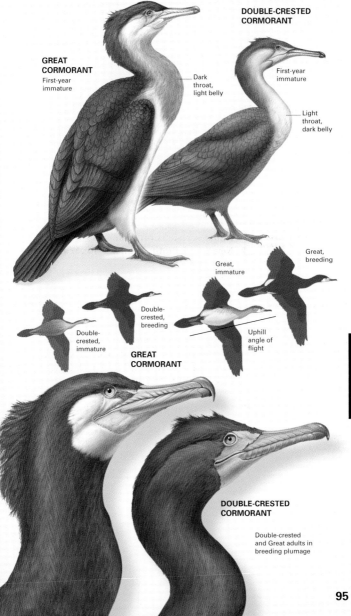

DOUBLE-CRESTED CORMORANT

GREAT CORMORANT
First-year immature

First-year immature

Dark throat, light belly

Light throat, dark belly

Great, breeding

Great, immature

Double-crested, breeding

Double-crested, immature

Uphill angle of flight

GREAT CORMORANT

DOUBLE-CRESTED CORMORANT

Double-crested and Great adults in breeding plumage

95

OSPREY AND NIGHT-HERON

Although not true seabirds, these species are common in and around harbor areas and offshore islands all along the Atlantic coast.

OSPREY
Pandion haliaetus

A familiar large bird of prey of coastal waters. In flight, wings show distinct "wrist" bend at leading edge. In summer, loud, high-pitched pleading notes of young and response notes of adults are common sounds. Fishes by plunging, talons first, into the water to capture fish. Breeds from Newfoundland to Florida. Winters from Florida south; scattered birds winter northward in mild winters. **Length:** 24 in. (61 cm). **Wingspan:** 64 in. (1.6 m).

BLACK-CROWNED NIGHT-HERON
Nycticorax nycticorax

A heron with bulky, hunched appearance. Often emits a loud "wock" call when flying to a feeding area at dusk or night. Normally feeds on small crabs and invertebrates. Sometimes preys on seabird nesting colonies on offshore islands. Active at dawn and dusk. Watch for this bird tucked in among breakwater rocks as your boat leaves the harbor. **Length:** 25 in. (64 cm). **Wingspan:** 44 in. (1.2 m).

OSPREY

Note the dark wrist patches and the leading edge angled at the wrist

Finger-like primaries are unlike the pointed wing of gulls

Adult

Adult Osprey

Juvenile
(first-year bird)
Very young Ospreys are flecked with white down

Adult

Adult

BLACK-CROWNED NIGHT-HERON

Juvenile
(first-year bird)

The hunched pose is characteristic of night-herons

BRANT AND EIDERS

There are no truly oceanic ducks or geese. However, some ducks are encountered well offshore as they migrate south or arrive on wintering grounds in bays and along island coasts. These sea ducks are diving ducks and at times can mass in remarkable numbers. The winter buildup of Common Eiders and Long-tailed Ducks in the waters off Martha's Vineyard and Nantucket, for example, can be spectacular.

BRANT
Branta bernicla

A small goose resembling a dark-necked Canada Goose. No bright chinstrap. The only "oceangoing" goose. At times can be seen well offshore. Favors Eelgrass (*Zostera marina*) in coastal bays but will also eat seaweed, in particular Sea Lettuce (*Ulva* spp.). A strong flier, often seen tucked into troughs of waves in migration. **Length:** 25 in. (64 cm). **Wingspan:** 46 in. (1.2 m).

COMMON EIDER
Somateria mollissima

Breeding
Winter
All year

A very large sea duck. Male has white back and chest and black underparts. Female light brown. Young male brown with white chest. Up close, note sloping forehead, black cap, and very long bill processes running up toward eye. Can occur in tremendous numbers. Flocks are often seen flying low over the water in long, undulating skeins. **Length:** 24 in. (61 cm). **Wingspan:** 43 in. (1.1 m).

KING EIDER
Somateria spectabilis

A spectacular sea duck. From afar, male looks half white (front) and half black (back). Up close, note soft gray head with showy, bright yellow knob on bill. Female golden brown. Usually seen not in massive flocks like Common Eider but as single birds or small groups of four to five ducks. **Length:** 18 in. (46 cm). **Wingspan:** 40 in. (1 m).

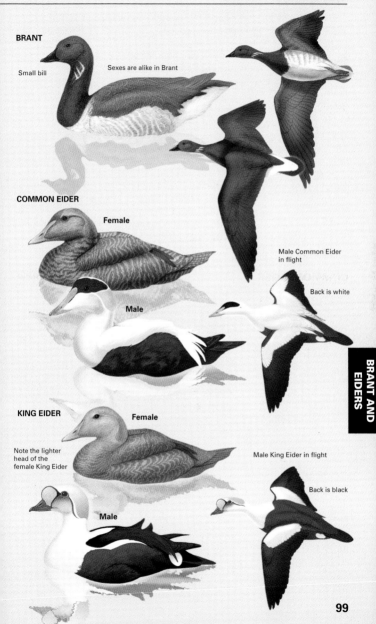

BRANT

Small bill

Sexes are alike in Brant

COMMON EIDER

Female

Male

Male Common Eider in flight

Back is white

KING EIDER

Female

Note the lighter head of the female King Eider

Male

Male King Eider in flight

Back is black

BRANT AND EIDERS

99

SCOTERS AND HARLEQUIN DUCK

These large, dark sea ducks spend their winters in coastal waters, sometimes many miles offshore. They dive to feed on mollusks and crustaceans. Their flight is strong, direct, and close to the waves.

BLACK SCOTER
Melanitta nigra

Male all black with bright orange-yellow knob on bill. Female brown with distinct pale cheeks, giving capped appearance. Forms small groups in winter along coastlines, but never in large rafts as formed by other scoter species. **Length:** 15 in. (38 cm). **Wingspan:** 35 in. (89 cm).

WHITE-WINGED SCOTER
Melanitta fusca

Male all black with white wing patch and white teardrop mark behind eye. Female brown with white wing patch and two dusky head patches at base of bill and on cheek. May form very large rafts off islands and coastlines. Perhaps the most common of the three scoters. **Length:** 17 in. (43 cm). **Wingspan:** 39 in. (100 cm).

SURF SCOTER
Melanitta perspicillata

Male black with distinct white patches on forehead and nape. Brightly colored bill. Female brown with dusky white splotches behind bill and on side of head and dusky patch on nape. Occurs in small to large rafts. Often swims with tail sticking up. **Length:** 15 in. (38 cm). **Wingspan:** 34 in. (86 cm).

HARLEQUIN DUCK
Histrionicus histrionicus

One of the most beautiful ducks. Male slate blue with rusty sides and striking white crescents on face, neck, and shoulder area. Female brown with tiny bill and distinct white patches at base of bill and on side of head. Loves coastal turbulence and choppy water off rocky outcroppings and island edges. **Length:** 16 in. (41 cm). **Wingspan:** 28 in. (71 cm).

BLACK SCOTER

Female

Male

WHITE-WINGED SCOTER

Female

Male

SURF SCOTER

Female

Male

HARLEQUIN DUCK

Female

Male

SCOTERS

BAY DUCKS

Bay ducks winter in sheltered bays and harbors along the coast, or in the lee of offshore islands. Goldeneyes are less marine in their habits but may be found in shallow coastal waters and estuaries.

GREATER SCAUP
Aythya marila

The most marine of the bay ducks. In flight, white wing patches extend well into outer flight feathers. Forms massive rafts of thousands up to several miles offshore. Dives to feed on shellfish in shallow water. Numbers have decreased dramatically in the past two decades. **Length:** 18 in. (46 cm). **Wingspan:** 32 in. (81 cm).

LESSER SCAUP
Aythya affinis

Very similar to Greater in all plumages but smaller, with more peaked head silhouette and smaller bill. It is often easiest to separate the two species by habitat: the Lesser favors inner harbors near shores and rarely moves far offshore. Any scaup more than a mile offshore is almost certainly a Greater. **Length:** 16 in. (41 cm). **Wingspan:** 29 in. (74 cm).

COMMON GOLDENEYE
Bucephala clangula

Male white with dark back and green head and white circle between eye and bill. Female gray with chocolate-brown head. Winters in sheltered coastal areas, sometimes in large flocks. Stays well inshore in bays and harbors. Winters south to Gulf Coast. **Length:** 18 in. (46 cm). **Wingspan:** 32 in. (81 cm).

BARROW'S GOLDENEYE
Bucephala islandica

Unusual. Male has white crescent at base of bill. Female almost identical to female Common Goldeneye. Favors same inshore habitats as Common, but southern limit of its winter range is Long Island. **Length:** 18 in. (46 cm). **Wingspan:** 32 in. (81 cm).

GREATER SCAUP

Female

Male

LESSER SCAUP

Female

Male

COMMON
GOLDENEYE

Female

Male

BARROW'S
GOLDENEYE

Female

Male

BAY DUCKS

LONG-TAILED DUCK
Clangula hyemalis

In winter plumage, white with dark chest. Male has exceptionally long tail plumes. In flight rocks from side to side, giving appearance of white (back) then black (chest). One of the fastest ducks in flight. Favors inshore waters and can form large, very noisy flocks. Huge rafts occur off Nantucket in winter. **Length:** 20 in. (51 cm). **Wingspan:** 28 in. (71 cm).

BUFFLEHEAD
Bucephala albeola

A very small sea duck with a rounded head and body silhouette. Male shows strong black-and-white pattern with black back, white underparts, and large white patch on head. Female a duller gray echo of male. Prefers sheltered bays and harbors and is usually seen in small mixed groups of four to eight males and females, not in large flocks. **Length:** 13 in. (33 cm). **Wingspan:** 21 in. (53 cm).

RED-BREASTED MERGANSER
Mergus serrator

A fish-eating diving duck with a long, serrated red bill. Both sexes have ragged crest at nape. Flight pattern is strong and direct, usually low over the waves. More marine in its habits than the similar Common Merganser, which favors fresh water. Favors sheltered bays, estuaries, and harbors. **Length:** 23 in. (58 cm). **Wingspan:** 30 in. (76 cm).

LONG-TAILED DUCK

Dark cheek spot

Female

Winter male has a white crown and neck

Male

In winter, both sexes have light heads and bodies with uniformly dark wings

Male

Noticeably smaller than other ducks

BUFFLEHEAD

Female

Relatively large head; strong black-and-white patterns

Male

Male

RED-BREASTED MERGANSER

Both sexes have a ragged crest

Female

Male

Slender body profile; typically flies close to the surface, in pairs or small groups

FLYING DUCKS – USUALLY CLOSER TO SHORE

COMMON GOLDENEYE — Male, Female

LESSER SCAUP — Male, Female

BARROW'S GOLDENEYE — Male, Female

BUFFLEHEAD — Male, Female

RED-BREASTED MERGANSER — Male, Female

LONG-TAILED DUCK — Male, Female

FLYING DUCKS – USUALLY FARTHER OFFSHORE

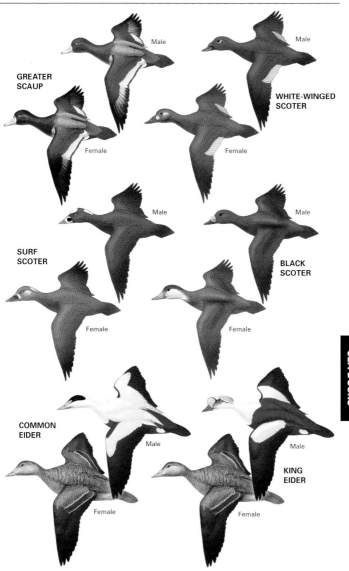

GREATER
SCAUP

Male

Female

WHITE-WINGED
SCOTER

Male

Female

SURF
SCOTER

Male

Female

BLACK
SCOTER

Male

Female

COMMON
EIDER

Male

Female

KING
EIDER

Male

Female

SHOREBIRDS

WHIMBREL
Numenius phaeopus

Breeds near Hudson Bay, moving to east coast in fall and returning along coast in spring. Although many Whimbrels winter along southern U.S. shores, others head to the Caribbean and into Central and South America. It may be these long-distance travelers that we see passing over wave tops well offshore. **Length:** 17 in. (43 cm). **Wingspan:** 32 in. (81 cm).

AMERICAN GOLDEN-PLOVER
Pluvialis dominica

A brown, stocky plover with short bill. Note the long, sharp-pointed wings, ideal for swift flight. Black underparts apparent in breeding plumage in spring. Travels in flocks. Very swift flight, low to the water. Migrating birds may be seen miles out at sea. **Length:** 10.5 in. (27 cm). **Wingspan:** 26 in. (66 cm).

PHALAROPES   These small shorebirds winter far out to sea, often in large flocks. Watch for fast-moving groups as approaching boats flush them from the water. These birds are susceptible to ocean storms. At times thousands are blown ashore, creating "phalarope wrecks."

RED-NECKED PHALAROPE
Phalaropus lobatus

Separated from Red Phalarope by distinct black streaking on back. Immature Red can show streaking but is never as contrasty as the Red-necked. Bill of Red-necked is needle-like compared to bulky bill of Red. **Length:** 7.5 in. (19 cm). **Wingspan:** 12 in. (31 cm).

RED PHALAROPE
Phalaropus fulicaria

A small bird with very fast, twisting flight. Separated from the Red-necked by all-gray back. All phalaropes have black "eyepatch" area in winter plumage. Bill much stouter than Red-necked. Buoyant in water, like a tiny gull. **Length:** 8.5 in. (22 cm). **Wingspan:** 13 in. (33 cm).

WHIMBREL

AMERICAN
GOLDEN-PLOVER

RED-NECKED
PHALAROPE

RED PHALAROPE

109

SKUAS

These massive birds are the top aerial predators of the Atlantic Ocean. Superficially similar to large gulls, they are very different in flight pattern and behavior. Bulky bodied, skuas are powerful fliers with deep, stiff wingbeats. Like jaegers, they nest on land near seabird colonies that afford them plenty of food for raising their young, then they spend the rest of the year at sea. Skuas do not flock – usually a single bird will arrive near a boat and harass all the other birds (including jaegers) for their food.

GREAT SKUA
Catharacta skua

Massive and barrel-shaped, with large head and short tail tapering to triangular end. Chocolate brown overall with large white patches at base of outer wing feathers. Flight is slow and steady, its power deceptive as this skua rapidly closes in on an escaping bird. A powerful hunter that defers to no other seabird. Very opportunistic; if it's edible, this bird will eat it. Skuas often chase Northern Gannets and flip them over in the air by hooking their wingtips under the Gannets' and pushing upward, causing the Gannets to crash into the water and disgorge their food. **Length:** 23 in. (58 cm). **Wingspan:** 55 in. (1.4 m).

SOUTH POLAR SKUA
Catharacta maccormicki

Large and bulky, similar in shape to Great Skua. Two color phases occur, dark and blond (light). Dark-phase body feather color more grayish than brown overall. Blond phase easily identified by very light head and shoulders. Both phases show large white outer wing patches. This skua is most usefully separated from Great by bronze-blond nape, visible in most dark-phase adults that enter our area and absent in all Great Skuas. South Polar Skuas in our area are nonbreeding birds spending the summer in northern waters, perhaps off Greenland and Grand Banks. **Length:** 21 in. (53 cm). **Wingspan:** 52 in. (1.3 m).

GREAT SKUA

Light adult

Intermediate adult

Dark adult

Back and wings are patterned with light feather edges for a "speckled" appearance

SOUTH POLAR SKUA

Light (blond) adult

Dark adult

Back and wings are more uniformly colored

SKUAS

JAEGERS

The "raptors" of the open ocean. Powerful and swift, these aggressive birds harass all species of oceanic birds. Three species of jaegers (German for "hunter") occur in Northern Atlantic waters. More falcon- or hawk-like than gull-like in appearance, jaegers are often recognized first by their deep, powerful wingbeats and aggressive behavior. Separation of the three species can be difficult, especially in young or dark-phase birds.

POMARINE JAEGER
Stercorarius pomarinus

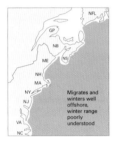

A heavy-chested, round-bodied jaeger. Two color phases, light and dark. Spatulate, twisted tail feathers make identification easy in breeding plumage. Young Pomarines, however, have small tail feathers that may look like those of smaller Parasitic Jaeger. Less white on outer wing feathers than in other jaegers; often only feather shafts show white. Distinct chest band in light phase. **Length:** 22 in. (56 cm). **Wingspan:** 48 in. (1.2 m).

PARASITIC JAEGER
Stercorarius parasiticus

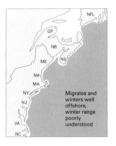

Two color phases, light and dark. Central two tail feathers stick out, forming a sharp ventral point, in full adult plumage. Both color phases have considerable white in outer wing feathers. Light phase has light gray sides that blend into white belly and lacks distinctive barring of dark phase. **Length:** 18 in. (46 cm). **Wingspan:** 42 in. (1.1 m).

LONG-TAILED JAEGER
Stercorarius longicaudus

The trimmest of the three jaegers. In breeding plumage the long (7 in., 18 cm) central tail feathers taper the body's appearance, almost suggesting a large, dark tern. No chest band, and very little white in outer wing feathers. The rarest of the jaegers off the Atlantic Coast, appearing only sporadically in migration, usually far offshore. **Length:** 22 in. (56 cm). **Wingspan:** 40 in. (1 m).

POMARINE JAEGER

Light adult

Dark adult

A massive bird, as large as a Herring Gull

PARASITIC JAEGER

Light adult

Dark adult

LONG-TAILED JAEGER

Light adult

Dark adult

Mantle is gray, not brown

A delicate bird, more like a tern in overall aspect; less aggressive than other jaegers

JAEGERS

SMALLER INSHORE GULLS

These gulls are seen in harbors and will follow a boat out to sea until land starts to fade from view, when they return to shore.

LAUGHING GULL
Larus atricilla

A trim gull with black head and deep gray back. Blood-red bill and legs. No white in wingtips. Note broken white ring around eye. In winter plumage, hood changes to dark patch at back of head. Immature shows black band at end of tail feathers. This gull's laughing call is a familiar sound from the middle Atlantic Coast southward, and the species is becoming more common in the north. Will follow inshore boats, "hanging" above the stern looking for handouts. **Length:** 17 in. (43 cm). **Wingspan:** 40 in. (1 m).

BLACK-HEADED GULL
Larus ridibundus

Very similar to Bonaparte's and mixes with that species. *Deep chocolate brown* (not black) head in breeding plumage. Blood-red bill and legs. Lighter gray back than Bonaparte's. Sooty gray underwings. Legs much longer than Bonaparte's, allowing easy separation of the gulls in mixed flocks. **Length:** 16 in. (41 cm). **Wingspan:** 40 in. (1 m).

BONAPARTE'S GULL
Larus philadelphia

A small, almost tern-like gull. Very buoyant when sitting on the water. Black head in breeding plumage. Wings in all plumages show a distinct white wedge on outer edge. Blood-red bill, deep pink legs. In winter plumage, black hood is reduced to a black smudge behind the eye. A fall-through-spring visitor to the coastline. At times found well offshore mixing with true ocean birds. **Length:** 13 in. (33 cm). **Wingspan:** 33 in. (84 cm).

LAUGHING GULL

First winter

Note the proportionately long wings

First winter

Adult breeding

Adult winter

Adult breeding

BLACK-HEADED GULL

First winter

First summer

Adult breeding

Adult winter

GULLS

BONAPARTE'S GULL

First winter

First summer

Adult winter

Adult breeding

SMALL, RARE GULLS

Small, almost tern-like gulls. The uncommon Little Gull is a recent immigrant from the Old World now breeding in the Great Lakes. Ross's and Ivory Gulls are very rare vagrants from the high Arctic.

LITTLE GULL
Larus minutus

The smallest North American gull. Like a small, short-legged version of Bonaparte's. Note black hood extending to base of nape in breeding plumage. Black bill, orange legs. In flight, lacks extensive white on outer wings and has dark gray underwings. Distinguished by tiny size and very short legs when standing with Bonaparte's and Black-Headed. Mixes with Bonaparte's in fall and winter off the coast. **Length:** 11 in. (28 cm). **Wingspan:** 24 in. (61 cm).

ROSS'S GULL
Rhodostethia rosea

Very rare. A beautiful gull, almost tern-like in form and action. In breeding plumage, note rich rosy bloom on chest and distinct thin, black band running around chin and up to back of the head. Very pale white or gray back. Note wedge-shaped tail. In nonbreeding plumage, Ross's is identified by its dove-like head and wedge-shaped tail. When standing, the long wings cross at the tips beyond the tail. **Length:** 13 in. (33 cm). **Wingspan:** 33 in. (84 cm).

IVORY GULL
Pagophila eburnea

Very rare in our area. Unmistakable in all plumages. Adult pure snow-white with yellow-tipped black bill. Black feet. Immature white with heavy spotting and sooty, smudged face. When the Ivory appears with other gulls, it looks like a ghost. Stays at edge of northern pack ice most of its life. Feeds with other gulls. When appearing in our area tends to be a coastal species. **Length:** 17 in. (43 cm). **Wingspan:** 37 in. (94 cm).

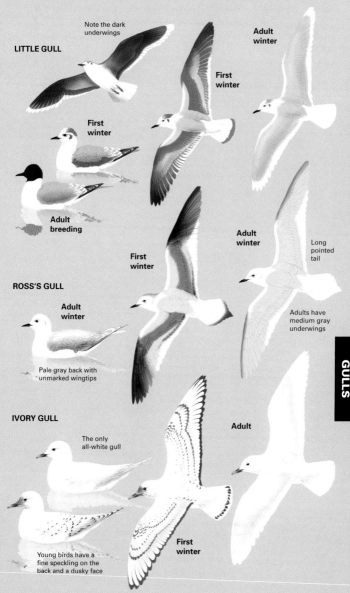

LITTLE GULL

Note the dark underwings

First winter

Adult winter

First winter

Adult breeding

ROSS'S GULL

Adult winter

First winter

Adult winter

Long pointed tail

Adults have medium gray underwings

Pale gray back with unmarked wingtips

IVORY GULL

The only all-white gull

Adult

Young birds have a fine speckling on the back and a dusky face

First winter

GULLS

SMALL PELAGIC GULLS

Two gull species are true ocean wanderers off the eastern seaboard. After breeding in the Arctic and along the far northern coasts they wander out to sea to spend the winter. Severe storms on the Atlantic occasionally drive these birds inshore with coastline gull flocks.

BLACK-LEGGED KITTIWAKE   *Rissa tridactyla*

A small gull with a dove-like head. Wingtips have a dipped-in-ink pattern that shows a clear edge contrast with gray back. Yellow, unmarked bill. Immature shows a striking dark **M** pattern across back and upper wings in flight. Black tail edge; distinct black collar on neck.

A gull that loves storm-tossed seas, often appearing in incredible numbers far offshore. Flies in circular patterns, rising in the air then dipping down to the surface level and riding up again. These large, looping patterns are diagnostic from a great distance. Follows boats until land is in sight. **Length:** 17 in. (43 cm). **Wingspan:** 35 in. (89 cm).

SABINE'S GULL   *Xema sabini*

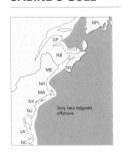

A beautifully patterned gull, the only gull with a forked tail. Note deep gray hood, black bill with yellow tip, and striking back pattern formed by black outer wing feathers contrasting with wedge of white on inner wing and deep gray back. Immature has a unique scale-like pattern on its gray-brown back.

A gull of the deep ocean. Rarely seen inshore except after severe storms. Buoyant when seen sitting on the water, its tail held upward. A strong flyer. Will come to chumming or activity of birds around a boat. Rarely seen; a standout sighting on any offshore trip. **Length:** 14 in. (36 cm). **Wingspan:** 33 in. (84 cm).

BLACK-LEGGED KITTIWAKE

First winter

First winter

Adult breeding

Adult breeding

SABINE'S GULL

First winter

Short bill with yellow tip

The only gull in our area with a forked tail

Adult winter

Bold wing pattern in all plumages

First summer

Adult breeding

RING-BILLED AND HERRING GULLS

These two similar species are the most common gulls of northeastern harbors, marinas, and inshore waters. The Ring-billed Gull matures over three years, the Herring Gull over four, leading to many distinct plumages for both species. Note the *substantial size difference* between the Herring and Ring-billed Gulls – the Ring-billed is considerably smaller.

RING-BILLED GULL   *Larus delawarensis*

A medium-sized common gull of harbors and shorelines. Easily identified by distinct ring around bill. Gray back. Greenish yellow legs. Black wingtips spotted with white; the black extends along the edge almost to the wing bend. Reaches full adult plumage after three years. Mixes with other gulls in harbors and in large flocks resting on breakwaters and sandy shores. Will follow boats, hanging in the wind just astern and looking for handouts. Will even drop down and take scraps from your hands. Does not follow boats far offshore. **Length:** 18 in. (46 cm). **Wingspan:** 48 in. (1.2 m).

HERRING GULL   *Larus argentatus*

An abundant bird; the gull most people think of when they think of "seagulls." Large, with gray back and black wingtips with white spots. White head and underparts. Flesh-colored legs. Yellow bill with blood-red spot on lower mandible. Yellow eye. In winter plumage, head is streaked brown with a dark eye line, giving the face a "mean" appearance. First-year immature is chocolate brown with lighter speckles. Herring Gulls reach full adult plumage after four years. Plumage may be distinguished by year of age until adult plumage is reached. Will follow boats. Sometimes ranges well offshore but is not truly oceanic. **Length:** 25 in. (64 cm). **Wingspan:** 58 in. (1.5 m).

RING-BILLED GULL

First winter

Second winter

Adult breeding

First winter

Adult winter

Adult breeding

HERRING GULL

First winter

Third winter

Second winter

First winter

Adult winter

GULLS

BLACK-BACKED GULLS

Only the Great Black-backed Gull is common on the northeastern shoreline. The Lesser Black-backed Gull, which has nested in Canada, remains a fairly rare gull that appears most often with inshore gull groups, especially in winter. The Great Black-backed is a ship follower and ranges far offshore. It is the first gull to breed each year, and breeding Black-backeds often prey on the eggs and young of other gull species.

LESSER BLACK-BACKED GULL   *Larus fuscus*

A European vagrant that now appears regularly along the Atlantic Coast. Best distinguished by yellow legs: similar Great Black-backed and Herring Gulls have flesh-colored legs. Very much like the Great Black-backed, but smaller than the Herring. Proportionately longer-winged than the Herring, but otherwise very similar in most immature plumages. Usually appears as a single individual mixed in with large flocks of wintering gulls. A coastal bird, rarely seen far offshore. **Length:** 21 in. (53 cm). **Wingspan:** 54 in. (1.4 m).

GREAT BLACK-BACKED GULL   *Larus marinus*

The largest gull of the shoreline. Jet-black back contrasts sharply with pure white underparts. White border shows from wingtips along rear edge of wings when in flight. Heavy yellow bill with red spot. Flesh-colored legs. First-year immature can usually be told by massive size and by pale head and rump contrasting with brown back and underparts. A common bird of harbor areas and shorelines. Of all the large inshore gulls, this species will follow boats out to sea the farthest. The Great Black-backed is gradually extending its range down the eastern seaboard toward Florida. **Length:** 30 in. (76 cm). **Wingspan:** 65 in. (1.7 m).

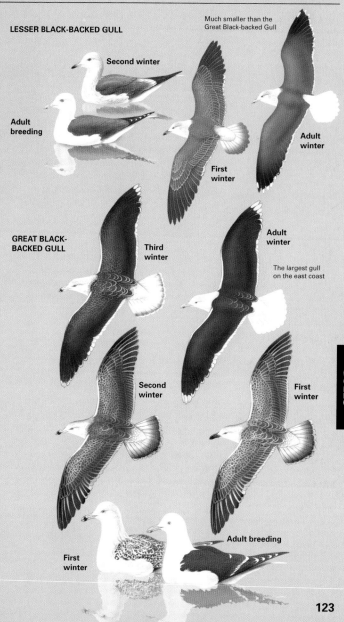

LESSER BLACK-BACKED GULL

Much smaller than the
Great Black-backed Gull

Second winter

**Adult
breeding**

**First
winter**

**Adult
winter**

**GREAT BLACK-
BACKED GULL**

**Third
winter**

**Adult
winter**

The largest gull
on the east coast

**Second
winter**

**First
winter**

**First
winter**

Adult breeding

GULLS

GLAUCOUS GULL
Larus hyperboreus

A large gull from the Arctic. Three distinct plumages, all without black in wingtips. First-winter plumage is pure white with pink legs and pink bill with black tip. Second-winter plumage is blond, again with pink bill with black tip. By the third winter, the adult-plumage bird has a gray back with white wingtips.

Wing length is important in separating the two white-winged gull species. In the Glaucous Gull, wings extend to the tail tip or just slightly beyond the tail, but not distinctly beyond it. In the Iceland Gull, wings extend well beyond the tip of the tail.

Though more of a coastline bird when it wanders from the north in winter, on occasion can be seen well out at sea, in mixed flocks with other gull species. Occurs far out at sea with greater regularity in the northern part of its range. **Length:** 27 in. (69 cm). **Wingspan:** 60 in. (1.5 m).

ICELAND GULL
Larus glaucoides

A large gull with all-white wingtips in all plumages. Smaller build than the Glaucous. Three distinct plumages. First-winter plumage is white with pink legs and thin, all-black bill. Second-year plumage is blond, again with thin black bill. By the third winter, the adult-plumage bird has a gray mantle with dark gray bands in wingtips. Wings are long, extending well beyond the tail tip. Mainly a coastal bird, but often mixes with offshore feeding flocks of gulls. Scan feeding flocks behind boats for this gull. It is more common offshore in the northern part of its range. **Length:** 22 in. (56 cm). **Wingspan:** 54 in. (1.4 m).

WHITE-WINGED GULLS

GLAUCOUS GULL

Second
winter

Adult
breeding

First
winter

Adult
winter

First
winter

ICELAND GULL

Adult
breeding

Second
winter

First winter

First winter

Adult
winter

GULLS

125

ADULT GULLS IN FLIGHT

All species are shown to scale

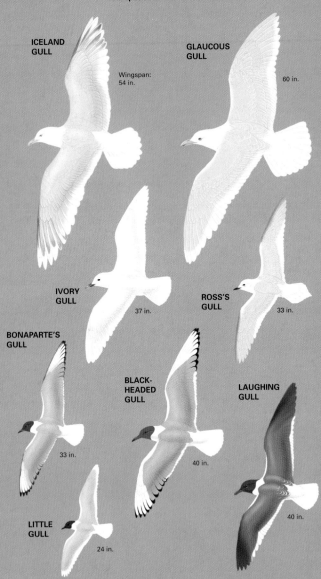

ICELAND GULL

Wingspan: 54 in.

GLAUCOUS GULL

60 in.

IVORY GULL

37 in.

ROSS'S GULL

33 in.

BONAPARTE'S GULL

33 in.

BLACK-HEADED GULL

40 in.

LAUGHING GULL

40 in.

LITTLE GULL

24 in.

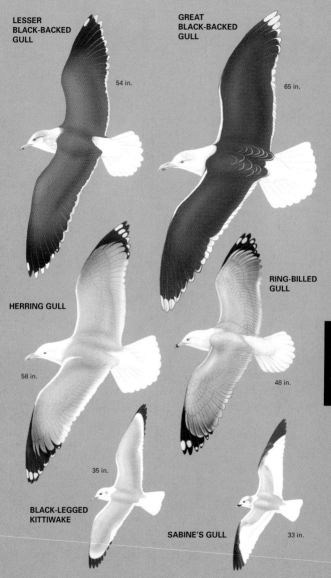

LESSER BLACK-BACKED GULL

54 in.

GREAT BLACK-BACKED GULL

65 in.

HERRING GULL

58 in.

RING-BILLED GULL

48 in.

35 in.

BLACK-LEGGED KITTIWAKE

SABINE'S GULL

33 in.

GULLS

IMMATURE GULLS IN FLIGHT

All species are shown to scale, in immature plumages

ICELAND GULL
Wingspan: 54 in.

GLAUCOUS GULL
60 in.

IVORY GULL
37 in.

ROSS'S GULL
33 in.

BONAPARTE'S GULL
33 in.

BLACK-HEADED GULL
40 in.

LAUGHING GULL
40 in.

LITTLE GULL
24 in.

LESSER
BLACK-BACKED
GULL

54 in.

GREAT
BLACK-BACKED
GULL

65 in.

HERRING GULL

58 in.

RING-BILLED
GULL

48 in.

GULLS

35 in.

BLACK-LEGGED
KITTIWAKE

SABINE'S GULL

33 in.

129

SMALL TERNS

Aside from the Arctic Tern, which is a true ocean wanderer, these are inshore terns. They are most often seen feeding in coastal waters, particularly near their breeding colonies.

COMMON TERN
Sterna hirundo

Our most common tern. Gray back and upper wings, white belly and under wings. Black cap extends down nape. Orange-red bill with black tip. In flight, gray wedge at center of back and darker wingtips. In winter plumage, white forehead and front half of crown. Immatures roughly follow adult winter pattern, with dark leading edge on upper wing. Very young birds are flecked with fine brown spotting. **Length:** 14 in. (36 cm). **Wingspan:** 30 in. (76 cm).

ARCTIC TERN
Sterna paradisaea

Black-capped with dark gray back and lighter gray below, producing a distinct pale line below the cap on the side of the head. Wingtips have a dark trailing edge when seen from below. More uniformly gray back than the Common. Blood-red bill. Very short legs, red feet. Immature lacks distinct brown cast of other small terns. The greatest migrant of all birds, departing the high Arctic and traveling to Antarctic waters during our winter, then returning to the Arctic to breed, an annual round trip of more than 23,000 mi. (37,000 km). **Length:** 15 in. (38 cm). **Wingspan:** 31 in. (79 cm).

ROSEATE TERN
Sterna dougallii

Uncommon. Pale gray to almost white. In breeding plumage, breast has a faint pink cast. Black bill with a deep red base. Long tail feathers form a deeply forked tail. In flight, wings are a clear, very pale gray. Outermost two primary feathers dark gray. Feeds in inshore waters. An endangered species, common only around its few remaining breeding colonies. **Length:** 15 in. (38 cm). **Wingspan:** 29 in. (73 cm). **Endangered**

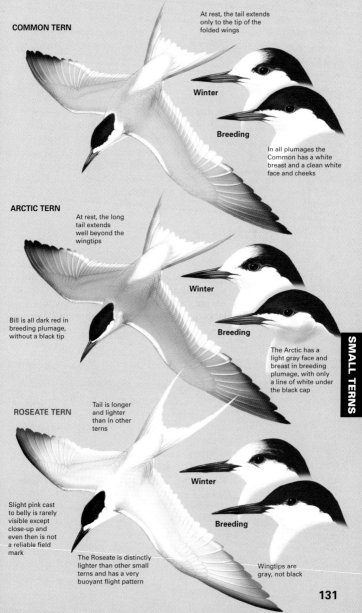

COMMON TERN

At rest, the tail extends only to the tip of the folded wings

Winter

Breeding

In all plumages the Common has a white breast and a clean white face and cheeks

ARCTIC TERN

At rest, the long tail extends well beyond the wingtips

Winter

Breeding

Bill is all dark red in breeding plumage, without a black tip

The Arctic has a light gray face and breast in breeding plumage, with only a line of white under the black cap

ROSEATE TERN

Tail is longer and lighter than in other terns

Winter

Breeding

Slight pink cast to belly is rarely visible except close-up and even then is not a reliable field mark

The Roseate is distinctly lighter than other small terns and has a very buoyant flight pattern

Wingtips are gray, not black

SMALL TERNS

Stay out of coastal and island tern colonies! Most tern populations are falling as these birds lose their breeding areas on beaches and coastal islands to human bathers and boaters. Terns are very defensive of their nesting sites. Disturbing their breeding areas causes high mortality, as chicks get lost and eggs get stepped on.

FORSTER'S TERN
Sterna forsteri

Similar to Common, but with pale wingtips and more orange base of bill. Wintering terns are easier to identify: Forster's has a heavy black eyeline, an all-white crown, and a gray nape. Other winter terns have a half-black crown and a black nape. **Length:** 14 in. (36 cm). **Wingspan:** 31 in. (79 cm).

GULL-BILLED TERN
Sterna nilotica

Pale gray with black cap and very heavy black bill. Stout, stocky body contrasts with sleeker Common and Forster's Terns. Black legs and feet. In winter plumage, head almost completely white. An inshore bird of salt marshes and bays. **Length:** 14 in. (36 cm). **Wingspan:** 34 in. (86 cm).

LEAST TERN
Sterna antillarum

The smallest tern. White forehead mark is present even in summer. The only tern with a yellow bill, tipped with black. Immature has especially noticeable dark leading edges on upper wings. An inshore bird; nests on beaches, and, in some areas, on flat rooftops near the shoreline. **Length:** 9 in. (23 cm). **Wingspan:** 20 in. (51 cm). **Threatened in some areas**

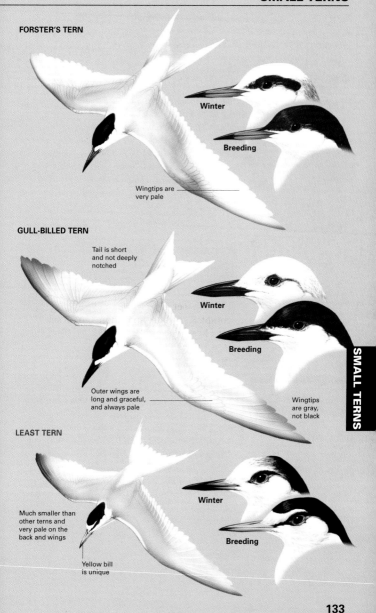

FORSTER'S TERN

Winter

Breeding

Wingtips are
very pale

GULL-BILLED TERN

Tail is short
and not deeply
notched

Winter

Breeding

Outer wings are
long and graceful,
and always pale

Wingtips
are gray,
not black

LEAST TERN

Winter

Breeding

Much smaller than
other terns and
very pale on the
back and wings

Yellow bill
is unique

SMALL TERNS

LARGE TERNS

Large terns are studied to best advantage along the coastline, where the birds stand on pilings or on the beach. All are southern species that wander north in summer. The Royal Tern is the species most likely to be seen well offshore.

CASPIAN TERN
Sterna caspia

A large, black-capped, heavy-billed tern nearly the size of a Herring Gull. Bright orange-red bill, with a tiny yellow area at tip. Wingtips dark below and lighter above, a reverse of the usual tern pattern. Shallowly forked tail. White-streaked forehead in winter plumage. Strictly a coastal species; does not wander far offshore. **Length:** 21 in. (53 cm). **Wingspan:** 50 in. (1.3 m).

ROYAL TERN
Sterna maxima

A large, sleek tern. Black cap with slight crest. Long orange-yellow bill. Pale under wings. Deeply forked tail. Unstreaked white forehead in winter plumage. Aggregates into large roosting flocks. A plunge-diver that feeds along inshore waters. Will sometimes follow ships at sea. **Length:** 20 in. (51 cm). **Wingspan:** 41 in. (1 m).

SANDWICH TERN
Sterna sandvicensis

A sleek, pale tern. Long black bill with a yellow tip (yellow tip may not show in young birds). Black legs. Black cap with slight crest. White forehead in winter plumage. Very similar in size and body pattern to the Common Tern, but with much lighter wings and wingtips. Rarely wanders far from shore. **Length:** 15 in. (38 cm). **Wingspan:** 34 in. (86 cm).

CASPIAN TERN

Winter

Breeding

Note yellow
bill tip

Light wingtips
above are dark
when seen from
below

ROYAL TERN

Longer tail than
Caspian

Winter

Breeding

Heavy bill is
all orange

SANDWICH TERN

Winter

Breeding

Long, thin
bill with
yellow tip

LARGE TERNS

DARK TERNS

BLACK TERN
Chlidonias niger

A fall migrant along the Atlantic Coast, usually seen in its winter plumage. Dark gray back and upper wings; much darker than other terns. All-black bill. Very dark red to black legs and feet. **Length:** 10 in. (25 cm). **Wingspan:** 24 in. (61 cm).

SOOTY TERN
Sterna fuscata

A large tern usually seen well offshore. Black upperparts contrast sharply with bright white underparts. Dusky gray underwings. The long wings are held high when gliding, with a characteristic sharp bend at the wrist. White-edged tail is deeply forked. White forehead does not extend past eye. Cannot land on water due to its poor waterproofing. Feeds by plucking prey from water surface with its long bill. A tern most likely to be seen in our area after hurricanes and tropical storms in the north. **Length:** 16 in. (41 cm). **Wingspan:** 32 in. (81 cm).

BRIDLED TERN
Sterna anaethetus

A rare tern from the Bahamas and West Indies that is sometimes blown into our area by hurricanes. Similar to the Sooty Tern, but lighter colored on the back, with a white collar at the nape. **Length:** 15 in. (38 cm). **Wingspan:** 30 in. (76 cm).

BLACK TERN

Winter

Breeding

Winter

SOOTY TERN

Black nape

Winter

Breeding

BRIDLED TERN

White collar

Winter

White extends over eye

Breeding

Back and wings are lighter than the Sooty Tern's

DARK TERNS

NODDIES AND BLACK SKIMMER

BROWN NODDY
Anous stolidus

A soft brown tern with grayish white crown. Long, thin black bill. Long, wedge-shaped tail unique among terns. Until Sooty Tern, doesn't wander north; rarely seen in our area except after hurricanes. Most Brown Noddies seen are immatures blown from nesting colonies in the Dry Tortugas off Florida. **Length:** 15 in. (38 cm). **Wingspan:** 32 in. (81 cm).

BLACK NODDY
Anous minutus

A very rare visitor from the Caribbean, sometimes blown north along the Atlantic Coast by hurricanes and other storms. The Black Noddy is a smaller, more delicate tern than the Brown Noddy, with a longer, thinner bill. **Length:** 13 in. (33 cm). **Wingspan:** 30 in. (76 cm).

BLACK SKIMMER
Rhynchops niger

A medium-sized relative of gulls and terns, with a unique long lower mandible used to "skim" surface waters for small fish. Dark, almost black back; white underparts. Huge bright-red bill with black tip. Most often noticed skimming across the surface of shallow coastal waters with its long lower bill slicing the water. Rarely wanders far from shore but often nests on offshore islands among or near tern colonies. **Length:** 18 in. (46 cm). **Wingspan:** 44 in. (1.1 m).

BROWN NODDY

BLACK NODDY

Cap is more diffuse than Black's

Longer, more delicate bill

BLACK SKIMMER

Adult breeding

Immature

ADULT TERNS IN FLIGHT

ARCTIC TERN

Wingspan:
31 in.

COMMON
TERN

30 in.

GULL-BILLED
TERN

34 in.

SANDWICH
TERN

34 in.

ROYAL
TERN

41 in.

LEAST
TERN

20 in.

CASPIAN TERN

50 in.

All species are
shown to scale, in
adult breeding (early
summer) plumage

ADULT TERNS IN FLIGHT

ROSEATE TERN
29 in.

BLACK NODDY
30 in.

BROWN NODDY
32 in.

FORSTER'S TERN
31 in.

BRIDLED TERN
30 in.

SOOTY TERN
32 in.

BLACK TERN
24 in.

BLACK SKIMMER
44 in.

TERNS

ALCIDS – RAZORBILL AND MURRES

RAZORBILL
Alca torda

A duck-sized bird. Black upper parts, white below. Often cocks tail upward while bobbing on water. This posture, combined with the deep, flattened bill, makes identification relatively easy. Stocky appearance enhanced by thick neck and by head carried tucked down. A winter bird of offshore waters. After nesting on cliff faces of North Atlantic shores, Razorbills wander the open oceans. May be blown ashore after fall storms. A deep diver that often stays down for extended times in pursuit of fish. **Length:** 17 in. (43 cm). **Wingspan:** 36 in. (91 cm).

COMMON MURRE
Uria aalge

The size of a small duck. Chocolate-brown (not black) back, white underparts. Thin bill often carried at an upward angle. In winter, cheeks whiten and a black line extends from behind the eye. Tends to fly in group lines when moving any distance. Occurs in large floating flocks off the coast. To escape approaching boats will typically dive rather than fly. In spite of the name, the Common Murre is the least common alcid in our area. **Length:** 17 in. (43 cm). **Wingspan:** 36 in. (91 cm).

THICK-BILLED MURRE
Uria lomvia

A little larger than the Common Murre, with a truly black back. Short, very thick bill, much heavier than the Common's. In winter, no white line behind the eye. The most abundant murre of the North Atlantic coast. As boats approach, usually flutters and runs across the surface, diving at the last moment. Nests in large colonies on sea cliffs in the Canadian Arctic and Labrador. Winters well out to sea, except when blown inshore after storms. **Length:** 18 in. (46 cm). **Wingspan:** 37 in. (94 cm).

ALCIDS – RAZORBILL AND MURRES

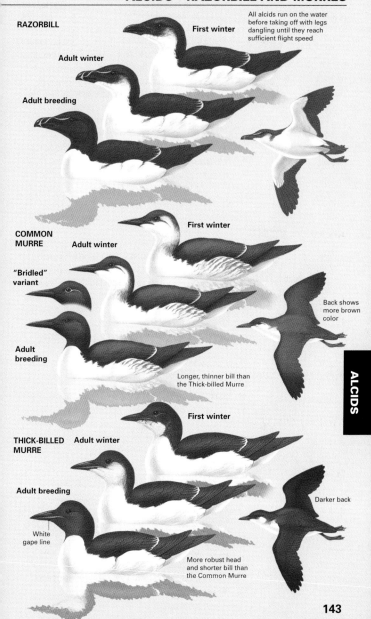

RAZORBILL

First winter

All alcids run on the water before taking off with legs dangling until they reach sufficient flight speed

Adult winter

Adult breeding

COMMON MURRE

Adult winter

First winter

"Bridled" variant

Back shows more brown color

Adult breeding

Longer, thinner bill than the Thick-billed Murre

THICK-BILLED MURRE

Adult winter

First winter

Adult breeding

White gape line

Darker back

More robust head and shorter bill than the Common Murre

ALCIDS

143

ALCIDS – DOVEKIE, GUILLEMOT, PUFFIN

DOVEKIE
Alle alle

The smallest alcid, about the size of a Common Starling. These black-and-white birds usually move with rapidly beating wings in small flocks, barely skimming the waves. Perhaps the most common alcid in the North Atlantic. Dovekies also provide food for gulls, skuas, and jaegers. These birds often fall victim to storms at sea, and many are blown onto land in seabird "wrecks." **Length:** 8.5 in. (22 cm). **Wingspan:** 15 in. (38 cm).

BLACK GUILLEMOT
Cepphus grylle

Breeding
Winter
All year

Unmistakable in breeding plumage. The only all-black alcid with large white wing patches. Plumage is grayish white in winter, but large white wing patches are still obvious. Occasionally found in large flocks, especially in feeding areas off nesting islands. More typically seen in pairs or as single birds. Tends to be an inshore alcid, often visible from land. Can dive for extended times in pursuit of fish. **Length:** 13 in. (33 cm). **Wingspan:** 21 in. (53 cm).

ATLANTIC PUFFIN
Fratercula arctica

The best-known alcid. Large, colorful parrot-like bill is unmistakable in breeding plumage and contrasts with white cheeks and white underbelly. No markings on wings. In winter, sheath of bill is dull gray. Young bird shows much smaller gray bill and dusky cheeks. In flight, the puffin's rotund shape and rounded wings with stiff flight make it fairly easy to identify. This is a bird of the rocky shore during breeding season, tucking its nest in among rocks or in short tunnels in turf. Winters far out at sea. **Length:** 13 in. (33 cm). **Wingspan:** 21 in. (53 cm).

ALCIDS – DOVEKIE, GUILLEMOT, PUFFIN

Puffins and guillemots fly in lines

Dovekies fly in loose flocks

Large white patches

BLACK GUILLEMOT

ATLANTIC PUFFIN

DOVEKIE

ATLANTIC PUFFIN
Winter plumage

Bill is dull colored or even gray in winter

BLACK GUILLEMOT
Winter plumage

DOVEKIE
Winter plumage

ALCIDS

FIN WHALE   *Balaenoptera physalus*

Description: A huge whale, dark gray to black on back and sides, with light gray or white underparts. Lower jaw asymmetrically colored: left side dark, right side light. Flippers and flukes small in comparison to body. At close range look for subtle chevron pattern of streaks from behind eyes to midline of back. Small, falcate dorsal fin sits far to rear, about three-fourths of the way back from jaw tip. **Red List – Endangered**

Habits: A sleek, fast swimmer despite its size. May approach drifting or very quiet boats but is indifferent to most vessels and apparently shy of engine noises. Sometimes performs low lunges across the water's surface while pursuing schools of fish; rarely breaches. Typical surface behavior is two to five blows, followed by a dive of five to ten minutes or more. Rarely rolls out its tail when diving. As their tails sweep up through the water, submerged Fin Whales often leave huge circular "footprints," formed by upwelling water, on the surface.

Similar species: The Sei Whale is smaller, has small oblong spots across the back, and has jaws that are dark on both sides. South of Virginia, Bryde's Whale has three ridges on the head and is much smaller than most Fin Whales.

Size: 30–70 ft. (9.1–21.3 m); average adult length 50–60 ft. (15.2–18.3 m).

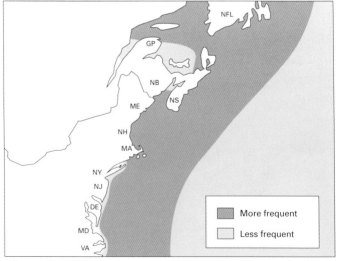

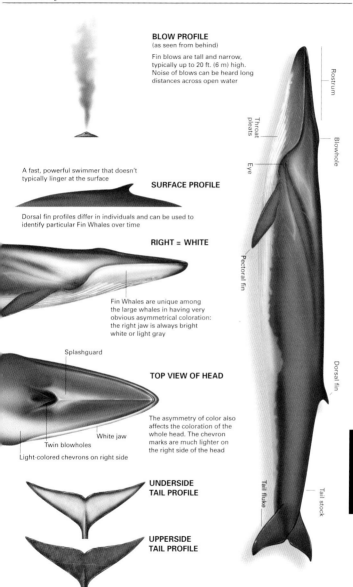

BLOW PROFILE
(as seen from behind)

Fin blows are tall and narrow, typically up to 20 ft. (6 m) high. Noise of blows can be heard long distances across open water

A fast, powerful swimmer that doesn't typically linger at the surface

SURFACE PROFILE

Dorsal fin profiles differ in individuals and can be used to identify particular Fin Whales over time

RIGHT = WHITE

Fin Whales are unique among the large whales in having very obvious asymmetrical coloration: the right jaw is always bright white or light gray

Splashguard

TOP VIEW OF HEAD

The asymmetry of color also affects the coloration of the whole head. The chevron marks are much lighter on the right side of the head

White jaw
Twin blowholes
Light-colored chevrons on right side

UNDERSIDE TAIL PROFILE

UPPERSIDE TAIL PROFILE

Rostrum

Throat pleats

Blowhole

Eye

Pectoral fin

Dorsal fin

Tail fluke

Tail stock

FIN WHALE

147

MINKE WHALE   *Balaenoptera acutorostrata*

Description: A small, fast-moving whale with a sharp snout. Its quickness and small size are often more suggestive of dolphins than any of the larger rorquals. Blue-gray, with distinctive light chevron marks on back. Belly light gray to white. Pectoral fins have white bands that are often visible under the water at close range. Falcate dorsal fin very similar to a dolphin, but positioned well to the rear of the back.
Red List – Near threatened

Habits: An inquisitive whale that approaches boats almost in the manner of dolphins. Often swims under or near moving boats but is generally shy and difficult to approach. The Minke's small size makes it easy to miss as it approaches boats, and Minkes often seem to appear suddenly from nowhere even when many whale watchers are aboard. Minkes breach more often than other rorquals; even so, breaching is infrequent. Typical surface behavior is five to seven nearly invisible blows, followed by a dive of three to eight minutes. The sharp snout (rostrum) often pokes a few feet out of the water as the whale surfaces.

Similar species: From a distance, may look like a lone dolphin or small toothed whale. Look for the sharp, dark snout as the Minke surfaces; it is unlike that of any dolphin or small toothed whale.

Size: 12–30 ft. (3.7–9.1 m); average adult length 18–22 ft. (5.5–6.7 m).

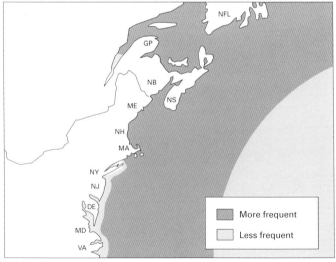

12–30 ft. (3.7–9.1 m)

MINKE WHALE

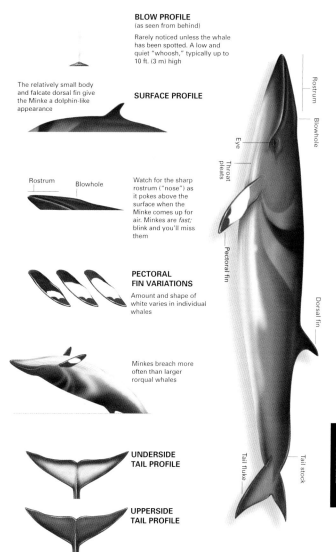

BLOW PROFILE
(as seen from behind)

Rarely noticed unless the whale has been spotted. A low and quiet "whoosh," typically up to 10 ft. (3 m) high

The relatively small body and falcate dorsal fin give the Minke a dolphin-like appearance

SURFACE PROFILE

Rostrum

Blowhole

Watch for the sharp rostrum ("nose") as it pokes above the surface when the Minke comes up for air. Minkes are *fast;* blink and you'll miss them

PECTORAL FIN VARIATIONS

Amount and shape of white varies in individual whales

Minkes breach more often than larger rorqual whales

UNDERSIDE TAIL PROFILE

UPPERSIDE TAIL PROFILE

Rostrum

Blowhole

Eye

Throat pleats

Pectoral fin

Dorsal fin

Tail stock

Tail fluke

MINKE WHALE

149

BLUE WHALE
Balaenoptera musculus

Description: A massive blue-gray whale with a proportionately small dorsal fin placed far to rear of back. Dorsal fin is often not visible until well after whale has begun to dive. The head, when viewed from above, is U-shaped and wide, with a large splashguard ridge just in front of the blowholes. The back is lightly mottled and may show a subtle chevron pattern behind the blowholes. **Red List – Endangered**

Habits: Generally shy; will dive or swim away when approached. The spout is very tall and narrow. A strong swimmer, the Blue can reach almost 20 knots when pressed. When diving, often rolls out its tail flukes a few feet above the water. Typical surface behavior is a blow every 20–30 seconds for several minutes, followed by a shallow dive of five to ten minutes. Favors coastal waters in the Gulf of St. Lawrence and Strait of Belle Isle and, in winter, deep waters near the continental shelf.

Similar species: A large Fin Whale may suggest the Blue Whale, but Blues are so much bigger that they are usually unmistakable when sighted. In diving, the Fin Whale dorsal fin is visible well before the tail stock rolls up, whereas in the Blue, the dorsal is placed so far back that it appears only just before the tail stock submerges.

Size: 30–100 ft. (9.1–30.4 m); adults now average 70–85 ft. (21.3–25.9 m), well under historical maximum sizes.

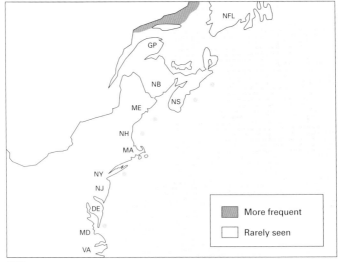

| | More frequent |
| | Rarely seen |

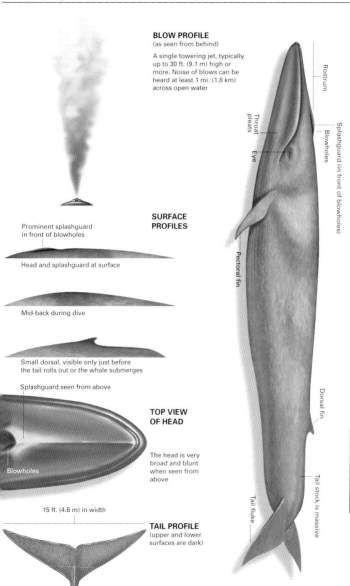

BLOW PROFILE
(as seen from behind)

A single towering jet, typically up to 30 ft. (9.1 m) high or more. Noise of blows can be heard at least 1 mi. (1.8 km) across open water

SURFACE PROFILES

Prominent splashguard in front of blowholes

Head and splashguard at surface

Mid-back during dive

Small dorsal, visible only just before the tail rolls out or the whale submerges

Splashguard seen from above

TOP VIEW OF HEAD

The head is very broad and blunt when seen from above

Blowholes

15 ft. (4.6 m) in width

TAIL PROFILE
(upper and lower surfaces are dark)

Rostrum

Throat pleats

Blowholes

Splashguard (in front of blowholes)

Eye

Pectoral fin

Dorsal fin

Tail stock is massive

Tail fluke

BLUE WHALE

SEI WHALE   *Balaenoptera borealis*

Description: A spotted blue-gray rorqual smaller than the related Fin and Blue Whales. The back, distinctly lighter than that of the Fin Whale, is typically marked with a sparse pattern of oblong spots. Head and jaws are dark on both sides. A subtle chevron pattern may be visible on the upper back and flanks behind the eyes. Dorsal fin is proportionately large, typically with a tall, falcate shape. Light gray or white belly. **Red List – Endangered**

Habits: Fast and erratic, often changing direction quickly when feeding and swimming in a zigzag pattern. One of the fastest whales, the Sei can reach a speed of 26 knots. A shallow diver, it skims surface waters for food. Rarely arches its back or rolls out its tail when diving. Typically reveals the middle of the back and flanks for longer than in other large rorquals, and when diving seems simply to sink below the surface. Often allows a close approach but then typically speeds away from boats. The Sei's natural history and distribution are poorly known.

Similar species: Very similar to the Fin Whale and, in southern waters, to Bryde's Whale. The Fin has a white right jaw, is larger, and is darker overall. Bryde's has three ridges on the head, whereas the Sei and Fin have one ridge in front of the splashguard.

Size: 22–50 ft. (6.7–15.2 m); average adult length 35–40 ft. (10.7–12.2 m).

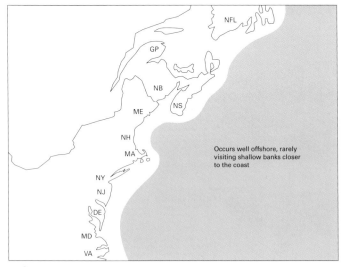

Occurs well offshore, rarely visiting shallow banks closer to the coast

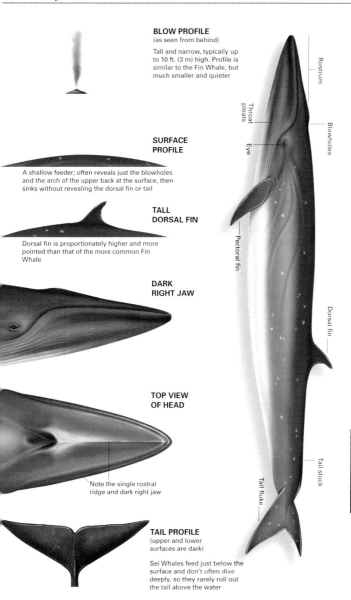

BLOW PROFILE
(as seen from behind)

Tall and narrow, typically up
to 10 ft. (3 m) high. Profile is
similar to the Fin Whale, but
much smaller and quieter

**SURFACE
PROFILE**

A shallow feeder; often reveals just the blowholes
and the arch of the upper back at the surface, then
sinks without revealing the dorsal fin or tail

**TALL
DORSAL FIN**

Dorsal fin is proportionately higher and more
pointed than that of the more common Fin
Whale

**DARK
RIGHT JAW**

**TOP VIEW
OF HEAD**

Note the single rostral
ridge and dark right jaw

TAIL PROFILE
(upper and lower
surfaces are dark)

Sei Whales feed just below the
surface and don't often dive
deeply, so they rarely roll out
the tail above the water

Rostrum

Blowholes

Throat
pleats

Eye

Pectoral fin

Dorsal fin

Tail stock

Tail fluke

SEI WHALE

153

Description: A blue-gray rorqual with three ridges atop head. Similar to the Sei Whale in size and coloration but restricted to warm waters. The three head ridges originate just forward of the blowholes and are the Bryde's most reliable field marks. **Red List – Data deficient**

Habits: Unlike the surface-skimming Sei Whale, this species is a deep diver and can stay underwater for 20 minutes or more feeding on fish and krill. In areas of cold-current convergence and upwellings, Bryde's Whales will feed in groups. Recent studies have shown a movement from inshore to offshore waters based on seasonal fish movement and plankton blooms. The deep-diving habit is reflected in the Bryde's surface behavior. After a deep dive its head will often surface at a steep angle, jutting well above the surface. When diving, it bends sharply, exposing much of its back, but it rarely rolls out its tail flukes. Sometimes displays curiosity and may approach boats.

Similar species: Look for the three head ridges: Sei and Fin Whales have only one. Very similar to the Sei, but in our area the Sei is most frequent in the North Atlantic in summer, whereas Bryde's rarely moves north of Virginia. The Fin Whale shows a white right jaw and is much larger and darker.

Size: 36–48 ft. (11–14.6 m); average adult length 40 ft. (12.2 m), smaller than the Sei.

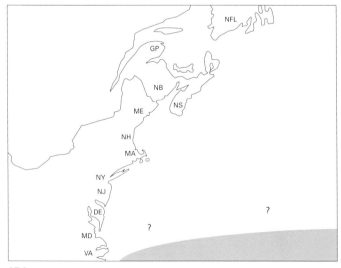

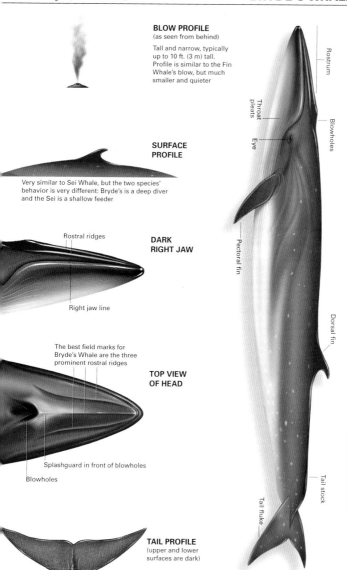

BLOW PROFILE
(as seen from behind)

Tall and narrow, typically up to 10 ft. (3 m) tall. Profile is similar to the Fin Whale's blow, but much smaller and quieter

Rostrum

Throat pleats

Blowholes

Eye

SURFACE PROFILE

Very similar to Sei Whale, but the two species' behavior is very different: Bryde's is a deep diver and the Sei is a shallow feeder

Rostral ridges

Pectoral fin

DARK RIGHT JAW

Right jaw line

Dorsal fin

The best field marks for Bryde's Whale are the three prominent rostral ridges

TOP VIEW OF HEAD

Splashguard in front of blowholes

Blowholes

Tail stock

Tail fluke

TAIL PROFILE
(upper and lower surfaces are dark)

BRYDE'S WHALE

HUMPBACK WHALE
Megaptera novaeangliae

Description: A large blue-black rorqual with very long, mostly white flippers. Variably marked on the head, belly, and tail with white or gray spots or patches. Top of head shows three rows of knobs, making a spy-hopping Humpback look like a giant black pickle. The tail is very wide, with a ragged trailing edge on flukes. **Red List – Vulnerable**

Habits: Highly inquisitive, readily approaches boats. The Humpback exhibits a wide range of sometimes spectacular social and feeding behaviors at the surface, including breaching, lob-tailing, and flipper-slapping. Humpbacks often feed in groups, where the whales cooperate to surround schools of small fish with "nets" or "clouds" of bubbles blown from their blowholes while underwater (bubble-netting). The blow is low and bushy. The Humpback often rolls its tail high out of the water at the beginning of a dive.

Similar species: At a distance may suggest the Fin or Sperm Whale. The Fin Whale rarely rolls out its tail when diving and does not dive with the sharp "hump" bending at mid-body like the Humpback. The Sperm Whale does roll out its tail like the Humpback, but its tail has a quite different shape and rarely shows light patches on the underside. The Sperm Whale has no dorsal fin.

Size: Average adult length 35–45 ft. (10.7–13.7 m).

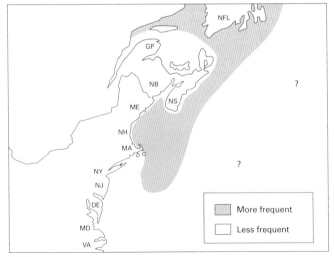

BLOW PROFILE
(as seen from behind)

Low and bushy, split left-right. May appear as a single jet when seen from the side. Typically 10 ft. (3 m) high

SURFACE PROFILE

The classic "humped back" profile, seen as the whale bends to dive deeply. Note wide variation in shape and color of the dorsal fin

PECTORAL FIN VARIATIONS

Mostly white above and below. Markings are unique to each whale

Flippers are often raised vertically above the surface and slapped down, apparently a form of communication

UNDERSIDE TAIL PROFILES

Patterns on the underside of the tail range from almost all white to almost all black. Each whale's markings are unique and persist throughout life, enabling scientists to identify individuals

UPPERSIDE TAIL PROFILE

Rostrum · Throat pleats · Blowhole · Eye · Pectoral fin · Dorsal fin · Tail stock · Tail fluke

HUMPBACK WHALE

NORTHERN RIGHT WHALE   *Eubalaena glacialis*

Description: Dark gray to black backs and sides, without any dorsal fin or hump. Most individuals in our area also have black bellies. The large white or gray callosities (wart-like structures on the head) are often apparent as the head shows above the water. These outgrowths are inhabited by numerous whale lice that sometimes give the callosities a pink or yellow-orange tint. Very large lower jaw line shows at sides of head when at the surface. Broad flippers with obvious finger structure visible. Uniformly black tail with very smooth, fine-pointed flukes. **Red List – Endangered**

Habits: When feeding this whale swims slowly at the surface with its mouth open. Often sluggish and surprisingly docile, sometimes suggesting the black up-turned hull of a sailboat more than a living whale. However, Rights can also be very energetic and acrobatic at the surface, breaching, rolling, tail-slapping, and spy-hopping. Often rolls its tail high above the surface when diving.

Similar species: Tail roll may suggest Humpback or Sperm Whale. The Humpback has a wide, ragged-looking tail usually marked with white patches. The Sperm Whale has a black tail with a different, more bluntly triangular fluke shape.

Size: Average adult length 35–50 ft. (10.7–15.2 m).

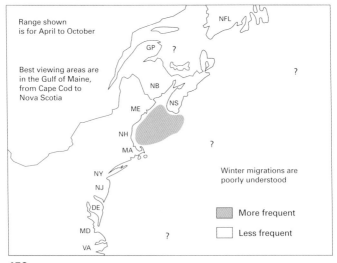

Range shown is for April to October

Best viewing areas are in the Gulf of Maine, from Cape Cod to Nova Scotia

NFL

GP ?

NB

ME

NS

NH

MA

NY

NJ

DE

MD

VA

?

?

?

?

Winter migrations are poorly understood

More frequent

Less frequent

BLOW PROFILE
(as seen from behind)

Thick and bushy, split when seen from behind or in front. Typically 15 ft. (4.6 m) high

The foremost upper callosity on the head is called the "bonnet"

Side view of head at surface

Typical "capsized boat" profile, with a smooth, unmarked black back and no dorsal fin

SURFACE PROFILE

When coming to the surface to breathe will show much of the head and the unique white callosities

White areas on the head are called "callosities"

Sometimes brings much of the head above the surface

PECTORAL FIN

When rolling at the surface will often wave pectoral fins in the air before slapping them down onto the surface

A single tail fluke poking up is sometimes the only visible sign of a Right Whale rolling at the surface

TAIL PROFILE
(upper and lower surfaces are black)

Often rolls the tail completely above the surface before beginning a deep dive

"Bonnet" callosity

Eye

Blowhole

Pectoral fin

Smooth back with no dorsal fin

Tail stock

Tail fluke

NORTHERN RIGHT WHALE

SPERM WHALE   *Physeter macrocephalus*

Description: A large, deep gray to black whale with a massive square head and narrow, many-toothed jaw below. No true dorsal fin, but a ridge of irregular bumps along the final third of the back. Pectoral fins are short and stubby. The skin looks wrinkled or corrugated. The blowhole is set at an angle on the left side of the top of the head, giving the blow a distinct leftward and forward projection. **Red List – Vulnerable**

Habits: Most commonly found feeding in the waters above submarine canyons and along the edge of the continental shelf. Often seen in groups moving at a surface speed of 4–5 knots. Swims at surface in a rhythmic pattern of 30–50 blows before diving, and then can be down for as long as an hour. The first exhalation after a long dive is very loud and can be heard over great distances at sea.

Similar species: May be confused with the Humpback Whale at long distances, but the square head profile and lack of a dorsal fin are distinctive. The Humpback has long white pectoral fins and usually shows white patches on its tail flukes when diving.

Size: 30–60 ft. (9.1–18.3 m). Sperm Whale populations today rarely reach the large sizes reported by whalers in the past. Adult male averages 50 ft. (15.2 m), female 35 ft. (10.7 m).

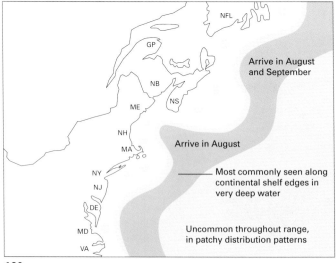

NFL

GP

NB

NS

ME

NH

MA

NY

NJ

DE

MD

VA

Arrive in August and September

Arrive in August

———— Most commonly seen along continental shelf edges in very deep water

Uncommon throughout range, in patchy distribution patterns

BLOW PROFILE
(as seen from behind)

Low and bushy,
projected forward and
to the left. Typically
7 ft. (2.1 m) high, but
larger males can blow
up to 15 ft. (4.6 m)

SURFACE PROFILE

Side view of Sperm Whale
surfacing. Note the blunt
head profile and forward-
angled blow

No true dorsal fin but usually a distinct "dorsal hump,"
followed by several smaller humps, or "crenulations"

TAIL ROLL

After breathing at the
surface for 10–20 minutes,
can dive for over an hour.
When preparing for a
deep dive, usually rolls its
tail high into the air as it
leaves the surface at an
almost vertical angle

TAIL PROFILE
(upper and lower
surfaces are dark)

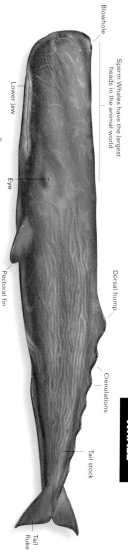

Blowhole

Sperm Whales have the largest
heads in the animal world

Lower jaw

Eye

Pectoral fin

Dorsal hump

Crenulations

Tail stock

Tail
fluke

**SPERM
WHALE**

161

LONG-FINNED PILOT WHALE *Globicephala melas*

Description: A medium-sized toothed whale, all black except for dark gray to medium gray "anchor" pattern on midline of belly between pectoral fins. Distinctive dorsal fin, low with very long base, especially noticeable in adult males. Dorsal fin is often hooked in older whales, which may also show lighter "saddle" mark just behind pectoral fin. Pectoral fins have a "wrist" bend, especially in mature individuals. Mature male has a very bulbous forehead profile. Female's head is also blunt but lacks the very rounded profile of the male.

Habits: A very social species. Most often seen in schools of 10–20 individuals, but may also appear in groups of hundreds. Favors cold waters near the continental shelf, well offshore. Though common, the Long-finned Pilot Whale's offshore habits make it an infrequent sight on coastal whale-watching excursions. Herds of pilot whales regularly strand all along the Atlantic Coast.

Similar species: Separated from the Short-finned Pilot Whale only by geographic range; Short-finned is rarely seen north of New Jersey. Pilot whales seen north of Cape Cod are almost certainly Long-finned.

Size: 10–20 ft. (3–6.1 m); adult male averages 17–19 ft. (5.2–5.8 m), female 13 ft. (4 m).

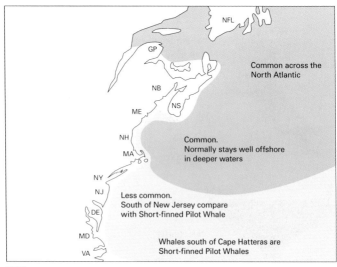

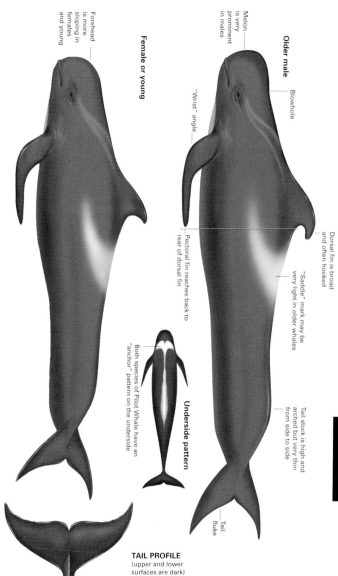

Female or young

Forehead is more sloping in females and young

Older male

Melon is very prominent in males

Blowhole

"Wrist" angle

Pectoral fin reaches back to rear of dorsal fin

Dorsal fin is broad and often hooked

"Saddle" mark may be very light in older whales

Tail stock is high and arched but very thin from side to side

Tail fluke

Underside pattern

Both species of Pilot Whale have an "anchor" pattern on the underside

TAIL PROFILE
(upper and lower surfaces are dark)

PILOT WHALE

SHORT-FINNED PILOT WHALE *Globicephala macrorhynchus*

Description: A near duplicate of the Long-finned Pilot Whale. Range is the key factor in field identification. In good light, look for a gray "saddle" mark behind the dorsal fin and more white in throat area than in the Long-finned. Pectoral fins are shorter in proportion to body size, and dorsal fin is typically higher and more falcate than in the Long-finned. The male's large, bulbous head grows with age. **Red List – Conservation dependent**

Habits: Most commonly seen in pods of 10–30 individuals, but some pods can be much larger. Mainly an offshore whale, occasionally coming near shore. Large groups are regularly stranded on the Atlantic Coast for unknown reasons. Thought to feed on squid in deep offshore waters and near-shore canyon areas, mainly at night.

Similar species: Can be separated from the Long-finned Pilot Whale only by geographic range; the Long-finned is rarely seen south of New Jersey. All pilot whales south of Maryland are almost certainly Short-finned.

Size: 9–18 ft. (2.7–5.5 m); adult male averages 17–19 ft. (5.2–5.8 m), female 13 ft. (4 m).

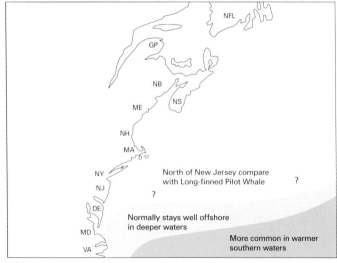

North of New Jersey compare with Long-finned Pilot Whale

Normally stays well offshore in deeper waters

More common in warmer southern waters

SHORT-FINNED PILOT WHALE

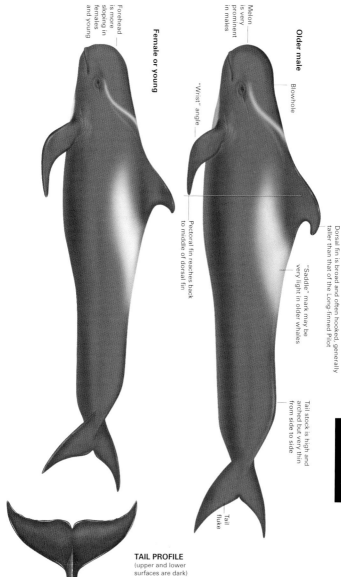

Older male

Melon is very prominent in males

Blowhole

Dorsal fin is broad and often hooked, generally taller than that of the Long-finned Pilot

"Saddle" mark may be very light in older whales

"Wrist" angle

Pectoral fin reaches back to middle of dorsal fin

Tail stock is high and arched but very thin from side to side

Tail fluke

Female or young

Forehead is more sloping in females and young

TAIL PROFILE
(upper and lower surfaces are dark)

PILOT
WHALE

165

FALSE KILLER WHALE

Pseudorca crassidens

Description: A very large dolphin. Relatively small tapered head, sloping forehead profile, and "wrist" bends in pectoral fins are the best field marks for this species. Mostly black except for a small patch of gray on chest between pectoral fins. Large teeth are often visible at close ranges.

Habits: Favors deep ocean waters and is rarely seen north of Maryland. The only "blackfish" species that rides bow waves. False Killers are never common in our area, but they appear sporadically in large groups that are very energetic and likely to be noticed if present. They breach, lob-tail, and spy-hop at the surface and are curious about boats. Reported to attack other dolphin species and sometimes young Humpback Whales.

Similar species: Slimmer and smaller-headed than the Killer Whale (Orca), and lacks any trace of white. Darker than all other toothed whale species except pilot whales. Pilot whales have large, bulbous heads and lack the tall, falcate dorsal fin of the False Killer.

Size: 9–19 ft. (2.7–5.8 m). Very large, comparable in size to the Killer Whale and pilot whales. Average adult length 15 ft. (4.6 m).

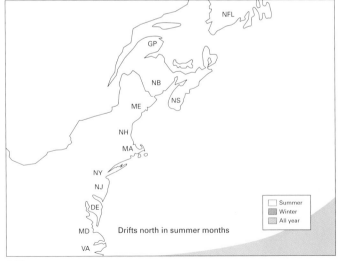

Drifts north in summer months

☐ Summer
■ Winter
▨ All year

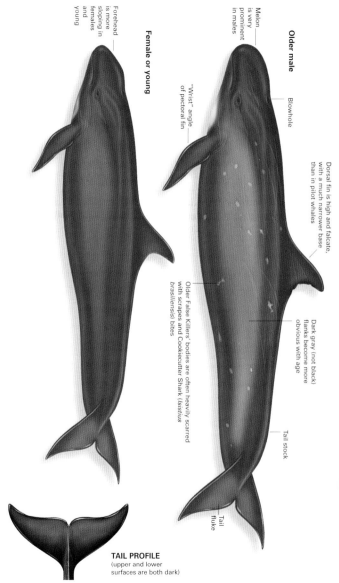

Older male

Melon is very prominent in males

Blowhole

Dorsal fin is high and falcate, with a much narrower base than in pilot whales

"Wrist" angle of pectoral fin

Dark gray (not black) flanks become more obvious with age

Older False Killers' bodies are often heavily scarred with scrapes and Cookiecutter Shark (*Isistius brasiliensis*) bites

Tail stock

Tail fluke

Female or young

Forehead is more sloping in females and young

TAIL PROFILE (upper and lower surfaces are both dark)

FALSE KILLER WHALE

167

SEPARATING THE "BLACKFISH"

"Blackfish" is the informal term used to describe these large black dolphin species. Our four blackfish all favor offshore waters, although they may sometimes be seen near shore. We have grouped them here for easy comparison. At sea it can be quite difficult to tell one blackfish species from another.

KILLER WHALE (ORCA) *Orcinus orca*

The white side patches and massive girth of the Killer Whale are the best field marks. Remember that females and younger Orcas of both sexes lack the huge dorsal fin of the adult male. Female dorsal fins are similar to the False Killer Whale's. The low, bushy blow is sometimes visible in cold air. **Red List – Data deficient**

FALSE KILLER WHALE *Pseudorca crassidens*

All black; never shows any trace of white. Much smaller and trimmer than the Killer Whale (Orca). Note the narrow pectoral fins, with distinct "wrist" angles and sharp pointed ends. Much more common than the Killer Whale, especially in waters south of Virginia.

LONG-FINNED PILOT WHALE *Globicephala melas*

The low, broad-based dorsal fin and bulbous forehead profile are the best field marks for this species. At sea it is almost impossible to separate the Long-finned Pilot from the Short-finned Pilot by sight. Note the "saddle" mark behind the dorsal fin, which grows lighter with age.

SHORT-FINNED PILOT WHALE *Globicephala macrorhynchus*

The proportionately short pectoral fins are the only useful field mark. The Short-finned Pilot has a more southern distribution, and *most* pilot whales south of New Jersey can be identified as Short-finneds. North of Long Island, the species will almost certainly be the Long-finned Pilot. **Red List – Conservation dependent**

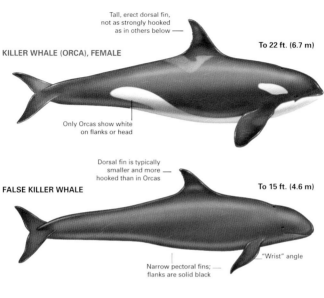

KILLER WHALE (ORCA), FEMALE

Tall, erect dorsal fin, not as strongly hooked as in others below —

To 22 ft. (6.7 m)

Only Orcas show white on flanks or head

FALSE KILLER WHALE

Dorsal fin is typically smaller and more — hooked than in Orcas

To 15 ft. (4.6 m)

"Wrist" angle

Narrow pectoral fins; — flanks are solid black

LONG-FINNED PILOT WHALE*

Low, broad-based dorsal — fin is very strongly hooked

To 20 ft. (6.1 m)

* Long-finned and Short-finned Pilot Whales are almost impossible to distinguish visually at sea. Note that they separate by geographic range (see maps on opposite page)

Long, narrow pectorals

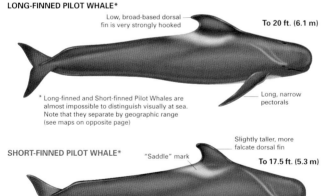

SHORT-FINNED PILOT WHALE*

"Saddle" mark

Slightly taller, more falcate dorsal fin

To 17.5 ft. (5.3 m)

Shorter pectorals —

White patch is more visible

GRAMPUS

Grampus griseus

Description: Also called Risso's Dolphin. A large-headed, blunt-faced dolphin reminiscent of pilot whales in general shape. Forehead is blunt and sloping, without a bulbous "melon" shape. Light gray body with dark fins. Perhaps the most diagnostic feature is the scarring that occurs all over the back and sides, apparently created by other Grampus while fighting. The network of scars on older adults makes their backs very light gray. **Red List – Data deficient**

Habits: Grampus favor deep warm water well offshore, such as the Gulf Stream off Cape Hatteras. Very active at the surface, where they breach, lob-tail, and spy-hop, often in large pods of 30 or more individuals. Grampus feed mainly on squid, and their underparts often show sucker marks. Although not common, they occur along the entire Atlantic Coast, drifting north in warmer months. Unusual but possible north of Cape Cod and the Gulf of Maine.

Similar species: Schools of pilot whales are often encountered in the same areas frequented by the Grampus. Pilot whales are much darker, have much more bulbous heads, and have dorsal fins that are much lower and broad-based than the Grampus. May be separated from other dolphin species by its overall coloration and blunt head shape.

Size: 8–13 ft. (2.5–4 m); average adult length 10 ft. (3 m) and weight 650 lbs. (295 kg).

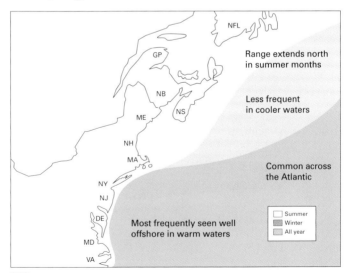

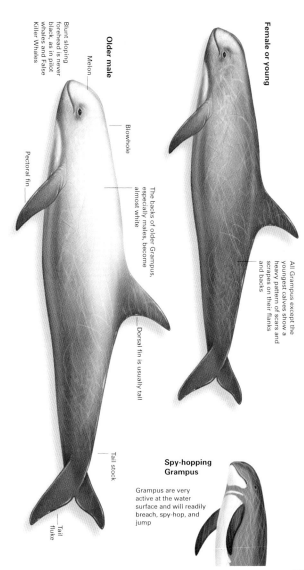

Female or young

All Grampus except the youngest calves show a heavy pattern of scars and scrapes on their flanks and backs

Older male

Melon

Blunt sloping forehead is never black, as in pilot whales and False Killer Whales

Blowhole

Pectoral fin

The backs of older Grampus, especially males, become almost white

Dorsal fin is usually tall

Tail stock

Tail fluke

Spy-hopping Grampus

Grampus are very active at the water surface and will readily breach, spy-hop, and jump

Description: The uniform, unmarked lightness of the Beluga is unique. The bulbous head is proportionately small. The back has a low dorsal ridge, not a true dorsal fin. The Beluga is also unique among cetaceans in having a clear separation between head and chest, often showing a neck crease or fold in front of the pectoral fins. The head is very mobile, possibly to aid in navigating under ice or in very shallow water. Newborn calves are brown or gray and become white as they mature.
Red List – Vulnerable

Habits: Often lolls at the surface, swimming slowly. In the wild, slaps its flipper at the surface, tail-slaps, and spy-hops but rarely breaches. At close range its whistling squeals and clicks can be heard through boat hulls. Often allows close approach and shows curiosity about boats.

Frequently seen in large pods in breeding areas along the northern shores of the Gulf of St. Lawrence, particularly near the Saguenay River in Quebec. Individuals have been spotted off the coast as far south as Long Island Sound, especially in winter. Favors coastal waters and rarely ventures far offshore.

Size: 10–15 ft. (3–4.6 m); adult male averages 13 ft. (4 m), female 11 ft. (3.4 m).

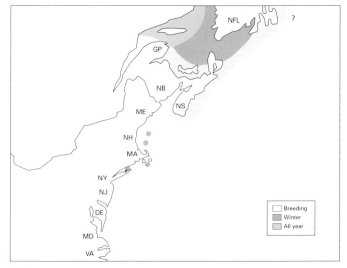

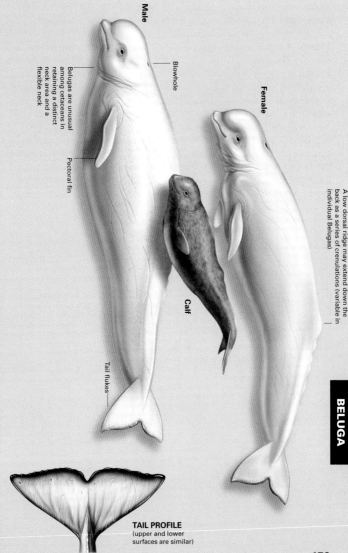

Male

Blowhole

Belugas are unusual among cetaceans in retaining a distinct neck area and a flexible neck

Pectoral fin

Female

A low dorsal ridge may extend down the back as a series of crenulations (variable in individual Belugas)

Calf

Tail flukes

TAIL PROFILE
(upper and lower surfaces are similar)

BELUGA

173

KILLER WHALE (ORCA) *Orcinus orca*

Description: Unmistakable at all but the farthest ranges. Deep black back is divided from almost pure white belly in a hard line, as is white patch behind eye. Dorsal fin of male may reach 6 ft. (1.8 m) in height and is often the first noticeable field mark at a distance. Body is much more massive than any dolphin species. **Red List – Data deficient**

Habits: An unusual but regular visitor to the North Atlantic Coast. Rare south of Long Island. Western Atlantic Killer Whales are much less well known than their Pacific Ocean counterparts. Thought to follow Bluefin Tuna populations along the Atlantic Coast and appears in the Gulf of Maine at about the same time as the Bluefins (mid-July). Known to attack Humpback Whales, whose tails often show Orca toothmarks.

Similar species: The female Orca has a smaller dorsal fin similar in shape to that of the False Killer Whale and to many dolphin species. The female Orca is always much longer and very much heavier than dolphins, and no dolphin in our area shows such bold white patches on the head and flanks. Pilot whales have no white patches, and their dorsal fins are low, often hooked over at the tip, and very broad at the base.

Size: 12–30 ft. (3.7–9.1 m); adult male averages 19–22 ft. (5.8–6.7 m), with a massive girth; female is considerably smaller and slimmer, averaging 16 ft. (4.9 m).

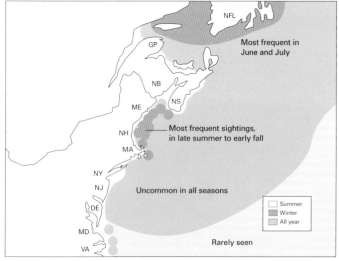

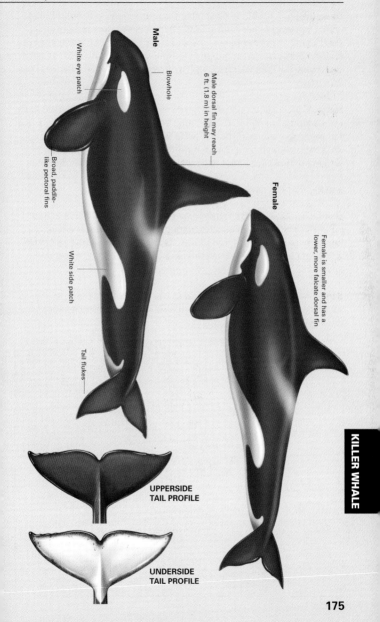

Male

White eye patch

Blowhole

Male dorsal fin may reach 6 ft. (1.8 m) in height

Broad, paddle-like pectoral fins

White side patch

Tail flukes

Female

Female is smaller and has a lower, more falcate dorsal fin

UPPERSIDE
TAIL PROFILE

UNDERSIDE
TAIL PROFILE

KILLER WHALE

175

NORTHERN BOTTLENOSE WHALE   *Hyperoodon ampullatus*

Description: A medium-sized whale, uniform gray on back and sides with a lighter gray or cream-colored belly. Jaws project to form small "bottlenose" below bulbous forehead. Small falcate or triangular dorsal fin. No central notch on trailing edge of tail flukes. Body often heavily scratched and scarred, especially in older males. **Red List – Conservation dependent**

Habits: Favors cold, deep waters over submarine canyons well offshore. Locally common in the "Gulley" area north of Sable Island, Nova Scotia, but otherwise sparse throughout the southern part of its range. Usually seen in small herds of a dozen or more animals. Known to submerge for long periods, feeding mainly on squid. Sometimes rolls out its tail flukes before diving. Often curious about boats and attracted to engine and mechanical noises.

Similar species: Sperm Whales favor the same deep offshore areas but lack the prominent falcate dorsal fin of the Bottlenose Whale. Sperm Whales are larger and darker and have a much more wrinkled appearance. Sperm Whale tail flukes are heavily notched along the entire trailing edge.

Size: A large whale, comparable in size to the Sperm Whale and to smaller Humpback Whales. Adult male length 19–29 ft. (5.8–8.8 m); female averages about 2–3 ft. (0.6–1 m) shorter than male.

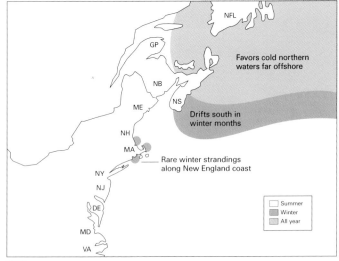

NFL

GP

Favors cold northern waters far offshore

NB

NS

ME

Drifts south in winter months

NH

MA

Rare winter strandings along New England coast

NY

NJ

DE

MD

VA

Summer
Winter
All year

Female

Male

Forehead of older whales is light gray or white

Back and sides are usually heavily scratched and marked with Cookiecutter Shark (*Isistius brasiliensis*) bites

Juvenile

TAIL PROFILE
(upper and lower surfaces are similar)

No midline notch in the trailing edge of the tail flukes

BOTTLENOSE WHALE

PYGMY AND DWARF SPERM WHALES

The behavior and natural history of these two closely related whales are not well understood. Both species may be more common than the sparse record of sightings suggests, because both are often stranded along the southern Atlantic Coast. The Pygmy is known from northern waters mostly by strandings; it is rarely seen north of Cape Cod.

PYGMY SPERM WHALE   *Kogia breviceps*

A very small whale, blunt-headed, with uniform gray coloration on back and sides and lighter gray belly. Very small dorsal fin. Small underslung jaw, as in the Sperm Whale. Only the lower jaw contains teeth. Note "false gill" marks behind and below eye. Inconspicuous; rarely approaches boats. May lie dormant at the surface and allow boats to approach closely. When startled, emits a cloud of reddish fluid from the anus and dives quickly. Sometimes leaps out of the water. Often seen alone or in small groups of up to 12 individuals. Sightings are uncommon, but the Pygmy is regularly spotted off the coast of North Carolina. Thought to prefer deep warm waters well offshore. **Size:** 9–11 ft. (2.7–3.4 m).

DWARF SPERM WHALE   *Kogia simus*

The natural history, range, and habits of the Dwarf Sperm Whale are poorly understood. Like the Pygmy Sperm Whale, the Dwarf favors warm waters well offshore, and the two species are almost impossible to distinguish in the field. The Dwarf has a much larger, more falcate dorsal fin. When these two species are stranded, the dorsal fin and "false gill" marks give them a shark-like appearance. Some observers have speculated that the gill marks may have evolved to make these two whales look even more like sharks and thus discourage predators. Like the Pygmy, the Dwarf Sperm Whale discharges reddish fluid from the anus when startled. **Size:** 7–8 ft. (2.1–2.4 m).

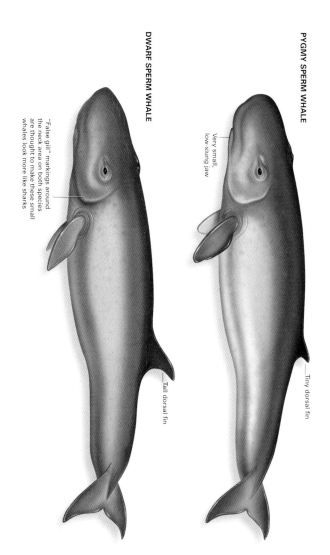

DWARF SPERM WHALE

"False gill" markings around the neck area on both species are thought to make these small whales look more like sharks

Tall dorsal fin

PYGMY SPERM WHALE

Very small, low-slung jaw

Tiny dorsal fin

SPERM WHALES

BEAKED WHALES

The medium-sized whales in this fairly large genus are rarely seen and are poorly understood. In true beaked whales, the male possesses an odd, enlarged tooth ("beak") that appears a fourth to halfway along the jaw and sticks out beside the upper jaw. The occurrence of beaked whales is unpredictable. These whales are so shy that the sound of an oncoming boat will cause them to flee. At sea they are inconspicuous and very difficult to identify and classify.

BLAINVILLE'S BEAKED WHALE   *Mesoplodon densirostris*

Sometimes called Dense-beaked Whale. Male has a large, curled jaw with a tooth protruding from its ridge at the halfway point. Elongated rostrum. Flippers far to the front. Probably common but very shy of boats. Mainly a tropical species, but individuals wander north with the Gulf Stream. **Size:** Average adult length 15–20 ft. (4.6–6.1 m). **Red List – Data deficient**

TRUE'S BEAKED WHALE   *Mesoplodon mirus*

Small head, short beak, and bulging forehead. Flippers far to the front. Unlike other beaked whales, tail fluke has central notch. Seen regularly off the Carolinas, but lack of sightings elsewhere may be due to the shyness of the species, not its rarity. Feeds mainly on squid. **Size:** Average adult length 16–18 ft. (4.9–5.5 m). **Red List – Data deficient**

SOWERBY'S BEAKED WHALE   *Mesoplodon bidens*

Unusual in the western North Atlantic; more common in northern European waters. Dorsal fin variable in shape. Known primarily from beached specimens. Most beaked whales prefer deep water, but this species seems to enter coastal waters more readily. Feeds mainly on squid. **Size:** Average adult length 15–20 ft. (4.6–6.1 m). **Red List – Data deficient**

15–20 ft. (4.6–6.1 m)

BEAKED WHALES

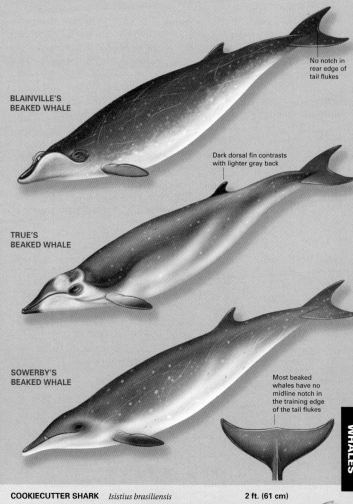

BLAINVILLE'S BEAKED WHALE

No notch in rear edge of tail flukes

Dark dorsal fin contrasts with lighter gray back

TRUE'S BEAKED WHALE

SOWERBY'S BEAKED WHALE

Most beaked whales have no midline notch in the training edge of the tail flukes

BEAKED WHALES

COOKIECUTTER SHARK *Isistius brasiliensis*   2 ft. (61 cm)

In warmer waters, the tiny Cookiecutter Shark plagues large fish and whales by taking small circular bites from their sides, leaving the round, light scars so commonly seen on many whale species

CUVIER'S BEAKED WHALE   *Ziphius cavirostris*

Description: Formerly known as the Goosebeaked Whale. The most common beaked whale, especially south of Long Island Sound. White forehead and back in front of dorsal fin. Dorsal fin small, falcate, variable in shape and size, and located behind the midpoint of the back. Color varies from brown or tan to slate gray. Only males have two teeth at tip of the lower jaw. Cuvier's Beaked Whales will roll out their tail flukes before beginning a deep dive. **Red List – Data deficient**

Habits: Often seen in groups of 10–25 individuals, primarily in offshore waters. Frequent strandings, especially along the southeastern Atlantic Coast, may indicate that Cuvier's approaches shallow water more often than other beaked whales or could be a direct measure of the whale's abundance. Apparently a deep diver; can stay down from 20–40 minutes. Feeds primarily on squid.

Similar species: Minke Whales are similar in size and surface behavior but are much darker and show a dark, pointed head profile quite unlike that of the beaked whales. No other beaked whales show the light or white forehead seen in adult males.

Size: Much larger than dolphins and most other beaked whales; average adult length 18–24 ft. (5.5–7.3 m).

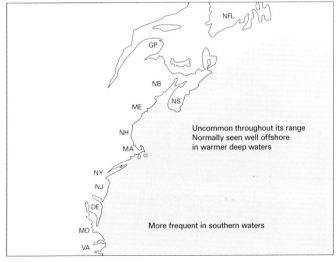

Uncommon throughout its range
Normally seen well offshore
in warmer deep waters

More frequent in southern waters

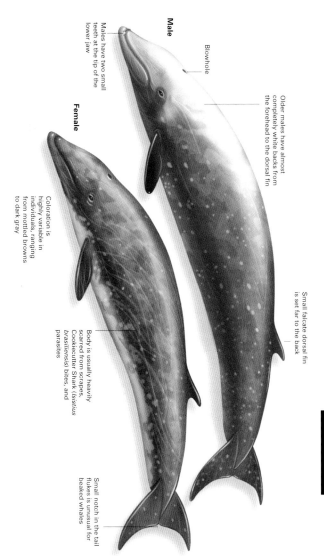

Male

Blowhole

Males have two small teeth at the tip of the lower jaw

Older males have almost completely white backs from the forehead to the dorsal fin

Small falcate dorsal fin is set far to the back

Female

Coloration is highly variable in individuals, ranging from mottled browns to dark gray

Body is usually heavily scarred from scrapes, Cookiecutter Shark (*Isistius brasiliensis*) bites, and parasites

Small notch in the tail flukes is unusual for beaked whales

BEAKED WHALES

183

ATLANTIC WHITE-SIDED, WHITE-BEAKED DOLPHINS

Our two species of "Lag" (*Lagenorhynchus*) dolphins separate roughly by range, with a large area of overlap in the Gulf of Maine and the Scotian Shelf: the White-sided is more common south of Nova Scotia, and the White-beaked is more common from Nova Scotia north.

ATLANTIC WHITE-SIDED DOLPHIN   *Lagenorhynchus acutus*

A dark, medium-sized dolphin with bold black, white, and mustard-yellow flank markings. Unmistakable at close range. Note that the beak is always dark and that the area behind the dorsal fin is dark with a bright mustard-yellow patch. Unlike the smudgy, indistinct flank patches of the closely related White-beaked Dolphin, flank markings are sharply delineated and more contrasting. Common in the Gulf of Maine in deeper waters (150 ft. [48 m] or more), rarely venturing near shore except in strandings. Rarely rides bows, but very active at the surface, often jumping and tail-lobbing. Usually spotted near feeding groups of whales and seabirds. Common from Labrador to Cape Cod. Spotty occurrences south of Cape Cod to Maryland. **Size:** Average male length 7–9 ft. (2.1–2.7 m), female 6–7 ft. (1.8–2.1 m). **Red List – Data deficient**

WHITE-BEAKED DOLPHIN   *Lagenorhynchus albirostris*

A dark gray dolphin with smudgy light gray flank patches. White beak can often be seen, but light gray flank patches are a better field mark. Sides of tail stock show a gray to almost white flash when diving, unlike the similar White-sided Dolphin, which shows a yellow flash just forward of the tail. A more northern distribution than the White-sided; more common north of the Gulf of Maine. Very rare south of Cape Cod. Feeds mainly on squid, although White-beakeds will also take fish. **Size:** Average adult length 8–10 ft. (2.4–3 m). **Red List – Conservation dependent**

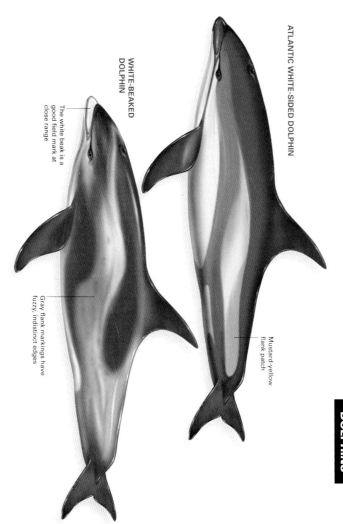

ATLANTIC WHITE-SIDED DOLPHIN

WHITE-BEAKED DOLPHIN

The white beak is a good field mark at close range

Gray flank markings have fuzzy, indistinct edges

Mustard-yellow flank patch

BEAKED DOLPHINS

185

SPOTTED DOLPHINS   *Stenella* spp.

Description: These two very similar species of *Stenella* dolphins are difficult to distinguish at sea. Young spotted dolphins of both species are unmarked and may be confused with the similar spinner dolphins. Mature spotted dolphins show a distinct spotted pattern on the flanks and back that increases in contrast and complexity with age. Older spotted dolphins often have bellies that are almost as darkly spotted as their backs and backs so spotted that they are almost light gray. When seen underwater from a boat, as when the dolphins are bow-riding, spotted dolphins often show a slight purple or violet coloration.

Habits: These are true pelagic dolphins that favor deep tropical waters well offshore. Both species are fast, high-energy swimmers that often leap high out of the water and readily ride the bow waves of ships. They are thought to feed mainly on Yellowfin Tuna and squid but also take small schooling fish such as herring and anchovies. As in other *Stenella* dolphins, the spotted species are highly social and may appear in groups ranging from a dozen individuals up to herds of several thousand dolphins of various species (usually Spinner, Striped, and Bottlenose Dolphins).

ATLANTIC SPOTTED DOLPHIN   *Stenella frontalis*

Coloration is often lighter and less heavily spotted than the Pantropical Spotted Dolphin, but this is highly variable. Note the much lighter eye stripe. This species is unique to the tropical waters of the Atlantic Ocean. Very active at the surface, often leaping, lob-tailing, and bow-riding. Occurs from Long Island south but is never common in our area. **Size:** To 6–8 ft. (1.8–2.4 m). **Red List – Data deficient**

PANTROPICAL SPOTTED DOLPHIN   *Stenella attenuata*

Back coloration is often darker than the Atlantic Spotted Dolphin, but only in younger individuals. Older Pantropicals are so heavily spotted that the dark back–light belly pattern gives way to a uniformly gray spotted pattern all over the body. Note the heavier eye stripe behind the eye. **Size:** To 6–8 ft. (1.8–2.4 m). **Red List – Conservation dependent**

PANTROPICAL SPOTTED DOLPHIN

ATLANTIC SPOTTED DOLPHIN

SPOTTED DOLPHINS

SPINNER AND STRIPED DOLPHINS   *Stenella* spp.

These are the most acrobatic of all dolphin species, often leaping high above the surface and "spinning" with their characteristic spiral-rolling leaps. These dolphins prefer warm offshore waters and are often associated with other tropical species like the Pantropical and Atlantic Spotted Dolphins. All are thought to follow schools of Yellowfin Tuna.

SPINNER DOLPHIN   *Stenella longirostris*

Dorsal fin triangular and very erect, not hooked or falcate. Long, thin beak. Flanks show three distinct color bands: black back, gray sides, and light-colored or white belly. Dark eye stripe runs from eye back to pectoral fins. Lower jaw is uniformly dark. Otherwise very difficult to separate from the Short-snouted Spinner. **Size:** To 4.5–7 ft. (1.4–2.1 m). Red List – Conservation dependent

Breeding
Winter
All year

CLYMENE DOLPHIN   *Stenella clymene*

Once also known as the Short-snouted Spinner Dolphin. Poorly known, probably because it is so hard to distinguish from the Spinner Dolphin. Dorsal fin shows typical falcate dolphin shape. Beak is shorter and stouter than that of the Spinner. Lower lips and tip of lower jaw are black; rest of lower jaw typically is white. Otherwise nearly identical to the Spinner Dolphin. **Size:** To 4.5–7 ft. (1.4–2.1 m). Red List – Data deficient

STRIPED DOLPHIN   *Stenella coeruleoalba*

A deep-water species normally seen only far out at sea in warm Gulf Stream waters. There are occasional reports from Georges Bank and the southern Gulf of Maine. Look for the bold "bilge line" that runs from the eye to the anus area and the gray flank markings. Very active at the surface, porpoising, spinning, breaching, and bow-riding. **Size:** To 4.5–7 ft. (1.4–2.1 m). Red List – Data deficient

CLYMENE DOLPHIN

STRIPED DOLPHIN

SPINNER DOLPHIN

SPINNER AND STRIPED

COMMON AND ROUGH-TOOTHED DOLPHINS

COMMON DOLPHIN
Delphinus delphis

A beautifully patterned animal. Deep gray back with yellowish sides and white underbelly contrasting into gray flanks. No other dolphin has as complex a side pattern. Note also the dark rings around the eyes, dark line forward of the eyes, and dark beak. Found in large schools usually churning up the water as they feed or seemingly just "play." They frequently jump clear of the surface and readily ride the bow waves of boats. Locally common in warmer waters throughout the world, these dolphins can appear anywhere off the Atlantic Coast in just about any water depth. However, the largest groups we have witnessed have been over the upwellings around submarine ridges and in the Gulf Stream, well offshore in deep warm waters. In northern waters may be confused with heavier-bodied White-sided or White-beaked Dolphins. In southern waters may be confused with spotted dolphins or very energetic schools of Bottlenose Dolphins. **Size:** To 6–8 ft. (1.8–2.4 m). **Red List – Data deficient**

ROUGH-TOOTHED DOLPHIN
Steno bredanensis

An uncommon warm-water species, rarely encountered north of Cape Hatteras except in Gulf Stream waters far offshore. Uniformly dark back, upper flanks, and tail stock. Back color ranges from dark gray-brown to almost black. Lower sides and belly marked with mottling and spots of lighter gray to white. A smudgy eyeline extends back from the eye to the base of the pectoral fin. The low, sloping forehead merges smoothly into the beak without the crease at the base of the beak that is characteristic of most dolphin species. The teeth are marked with fine vertical grooves that give the species its name. **Size:** To 6–8 ft. (1.8–2.4 m). **Red List – Conservation dependent**

ROUGH-TOOTHED DOLPHIN

The low, sloping forehead is unique among dolphins

COMMON DOLPHIN

COMMON DOLPHIN

BOTTLENOSE DOLPHIN AND HARBOR PORPOISE

BOTTLENOSE DOLPHIN   *Tursiops truncatus*

Perhaps the best known of all cetaceans, based on its television and film exposure. The only large dolphin species that regularly comes near the shore. Runs along shallow coastal waters, readily approaching boats, and enters large estuaries, where they can be viewed from bridges. Neutral to dark gray on the back and sides, grading to a pink-white underbelly.

The Bottlenose is highly social. It often "porpoises" when moving quickly, rolling and jumping free of the ocean surface, and it frequently slaps its tail on the surface (a social signal among dolphins) before diving. Ranges along the Atlantic Coast north to Nova Scotia but prefers warmer waters. Often appears in the "fog zone" where the Gulf Stream and colder currents mix.

Size: A large dolphin, with an average weight of 400 lbs. (181 kg). Average male length 8 ft. (2.4 m); female 7.5 ft. (2.3 m). **Red List – Data deficient**

HARBOR PORPOISE   *Phocoena phocoena*

The smallest toothed cetacean in our area, with an average length of 5 ft. (1.5 m) or less and typically weighing only about 100 lbs. (45 kg). Often seen in small social groups of 10–15 individuals. Dark above and pale below, chunky with small pectoral and dorsal fins. Very common, especially inshore, but not often noticed because of its small size, quiet habits, and shyness around boats. Fast movements and a low, inconspicuous dorsal fin make the species hard to spot, especially in choppy waters, where they can easily disappear into wave troughs. **Size:** To 4–6 ft. (1.2–1.8 m). **Red List – Conservation dependent**

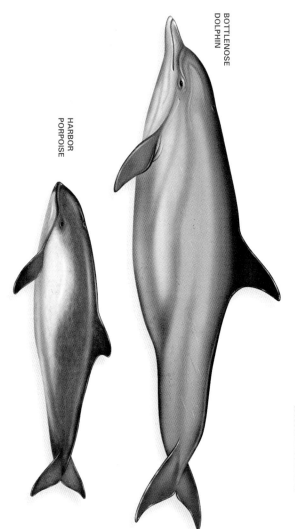

BOTTLENOSE
DOLPHIN

HARBOR
PORPOISE

BOTTLENOSE
AND PORPOISE

DOLPHINS

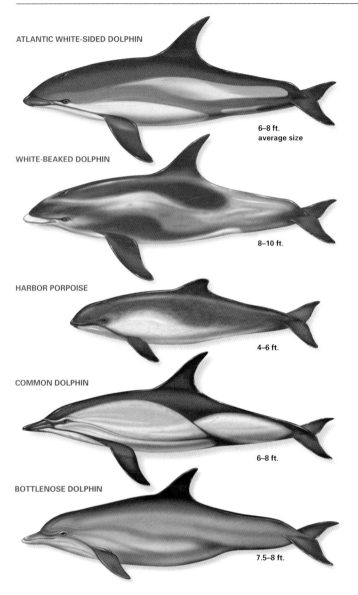

ATLANTIC WHITE-SIDED DOLPHIN

6–8 ft.
average size

WHITE-BEAKED DOLPHIN

8–10 ft.

HARBOR PORPOISE

4–6 ft.

COMMON DOLPHIN

6–8 ft.

BOTTLENOSE DOLPHIN

7.5–8 ft.

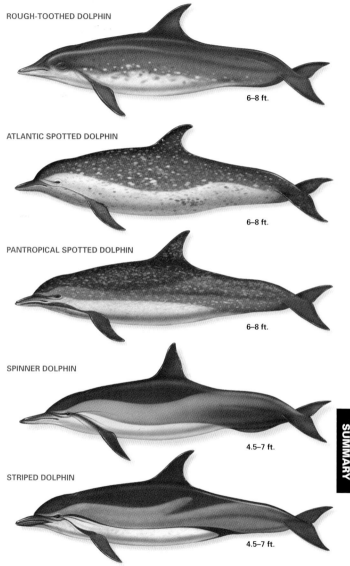

ROUGH-TOOTHED DOLPHIN

6–8 ft.

ATLANTIC SPOTTED DOLPHIN

6–8 ft.

PANTROPICAL SPOTTED DOLPHIN

6–8 ft.

SPINNER DOLPHIN

4.5–7 ft.

STRIPED DOLPHIN

4.5–7 ft.

DOLPHIN SUMMARY

HARBOR SEAL
Phoca vitulina

Description: The most common and familiar seal along the Atlantic Coast. Overall pelage (fur) color may range from light gray to almost black, with wide variations in the amount and pattern of spotting. Note that the color changes as the pelage dries: wet seals look much darker and grayer than dry seals. Head silhouette is very rounded, with a very short dog-like snout. Forehead slopes into the snout in a concave curve, unlike the heavy convex forehead of the similar Gray Seal.

Habits: Common in inshore waters from the Gulf of St. Lawrence south to Long Island Sound; much less common south of New York. Favors rocky breakwaters, small islands, and jetties as hauling-out points. Very playful and active at the surface. Sometimes shy, but may also be boldly curious and will readily approach boats. Watch for Harbor Seals' small, round heads spy-hopping at the surface.

Similar species: The Gray Seal has a longer, heavier, "horse-like" snout, whereas the short, rounded snout and concave forehead of the Harbor Seal suggest a spaniel puppy. The Gray Seal is also much larger and heavier-bodied.

Size: 3–6 ft. (0.9–1.8 m). Average length 3–5 ft. (0.9–1.5 m) and weight 150–175 lbs. (68–79 kg). Female is about 10 percent smaller than male.

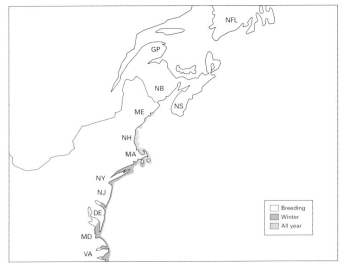

196

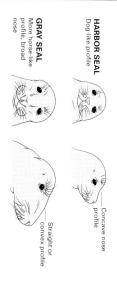

GRAY SEAL
More horse-like
profile, broad
nose

HARBOR SEAL
Dog-like profile

Concave nose
profile

Straight or
convex profile

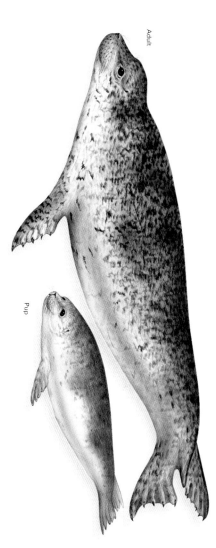

Adult

Pup

GRAY SEAL

Halichoerus grypus

Description: A large gray to black seal with a heavy, "horse-like" snout and a convex forehead profile. Pelage (fur) color ranges from light gray to brown or almost black, with wide variations of spot patterns within the population. Pups are typically white to pale gray with very light spots, darkening as they mature.

Habits: Favors colder waters than the Harbor Seal. Gray Seal populations are centered around the Gulf of St. Lawrence and are rarely seen south of Massachusetts. Prefers isolated rocky offshore islands, breakwaters, and jetties as hauling-out spots. This preference for isolated offshore haul-out spots makes sightings of the Gray Seal much less frequent than the less shy Harbor Seal.

Similar species: A good look at the head shape is crucial to separating our two common seal species. The Harbor Seal has a very short, dog-like snout and is much smaller and lighter than the Gray Seal. The pelage patterns of Gray and Harbor Seals are very similar and cannot be used to separate them. Gray Seals are typically much less curious about boats and humans than are the more gregarious Harbor Seals.

Size: 5–8 ft. (1.5–2.4 m). Adult male averages 7 ft. (2.1 m) and 800 lbs. (360 kg). Adult female averages 5–6 ft. (1.5–1.8 m) and 400 lbs. (180 kg).

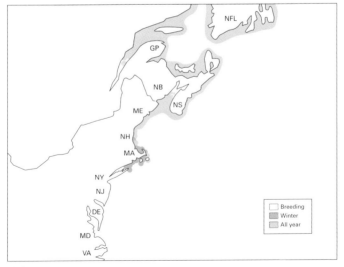

5–8 ft. (1.5–2.4 m)

GRAY SEAL

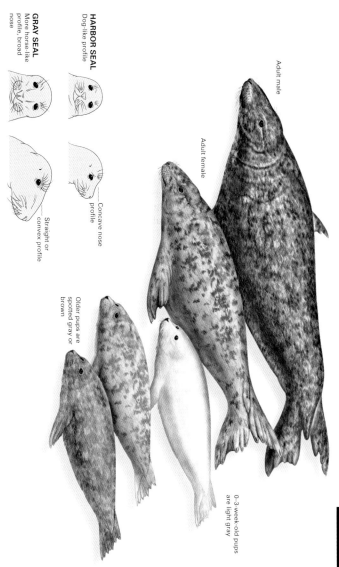

GRAY SEAL
More horse-like profile, broad nose

HARBOR SEAL
Dog-like profile

Concave nose profile

Straight or convex profile

Adult male

Adult female

Older pups are spotted gray or brown

0–3-week-old pups are light gray

NORTHERN SEALS

These northern seal species formerly were rarely seen south of the Gulf of St. Lawrence, even in the dead of winter. The Harp Seal has been regularly reported south of Cape Cod in recent winters, but the odds are still overwhelming that any seal encountered south of Nova Scotia will be either a Harbor Seal or a Gray Seal. Look for these three seal species, but don't expect to see them.

HARP SEAL   *Pagophilus groenlandicus*

A medium-sized gray to brown seal with a dark harp-shaped or saddle-shaped pattern on its back and sides. Older adults have lighter pelage and more contrast between dark markings and the silvery base fur color. Head is typically dark gray or brown. Range seems to be expanding southward. **Size:** Slightly larger than the Harbor Seal; adult averages 5–6 ft. (1.5–1.8 m).

HOODED SEAL   *Cystophora cristata*

A large seal with a heavily spotted pelage and black or dark gray face. Male has distinct "hood" nasal sac, which can be inflated in a threat display when the seal is disturbed. Favors deeper waters than other seals. **Size:** The largest seal in the western Atlantic; male to 9 ft. (2.7 m); female to 7 ft. (2.1 m).

RINGED SEAL   *Phoca hispida*

Similar to the Harbor Seal but smaller. Head and snout show a similar profile to the Harbor Seal, but the snout is more pointed in the Ringed Seal. Dark spots on the back pelage are typically ringed with a lighter halo, giving the species its common name. The most common seal in the Arctic, though rarely encountered south of the Strait of Belle Isle and Labrador. Favors ice packs at the shore margins but may also occupy ice floes far offshore. **Size:** The smallest seal species; adult averages 4–4.5 ft. (1.2–1.4 m).

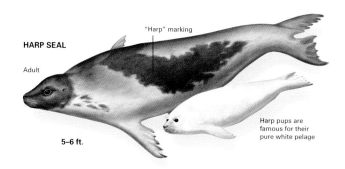

HARP SEAL

Adult

"Harp" marking

5–6 ft.

Harp pups are famous for their pure white pelage

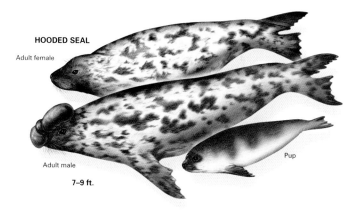

HOODED SEAL

Adult female

Adult male

7–9 ft.

Pup

RINGED SEAL

Adult

4–4.5 ft.

Pup

SPECIES CHECKLIST

PELAGIC ALGAE
__ GULFWEED *Sargassum natans* and *S. fluitans*
__ KNOTTED WRACK *Ascophyllum nodosum*
__ ROCKWEED *Fucus* spp.

JELLYFISH
__ BY-THE-WIND SAILOR *Velella velella*
__ LION'S MANE *Cyanea capillata*
__ MOON JELLY *Aurelia aurita*
__ MUSHROOM CAP *Rhopilema verrilli*
__ PORTUGUESE MAN-OF-WAR *Physalia physalia*
__ SEA NETTLE *Chrysaora quinquecirrha*
__ SEA WASP *Tamoya haplonema*

CTENOPHORES (COMB JELLIES)
__ BEROE'S COMB JELLY *Beroe* spp.
__ NORTHERN COMB JELLY *Bolinopsis infundibulum*
__ SEA GOOSEBERRY *Pleurobrachia pileus*
__ SEA WALNUT *Mnemiopsis leidyi*
__ VENUS GIRDLE *Cestum veneris*

PELAGIC INVERTEBRATES (PLANKTON)
__ ARROW WORMS *Sagitta* spp.
__ NAKED SEA BUTTERFLY *Clione limacina*
__ OIKOPLEURA *Oikopleura* spp.
__ PLANKTON WORM *Tomopteris helgolandica*
__ SALPS *Thalia* and *Salpa* spp.
__ SHELLED SEA BUTTERFLIES *Limacina* spp.

CEPHALOPODS
__ ATLANTIC BRIEF SQUID *Lolliguncula brevis*
__ GLAUCUS *Glaucus* spp.
__ GREATER ARGONAUT (Paper Nautilus) *Argonauta argo*
__ LONGFIN INSHORE SQUID *Loligo pealli*
__ NORTHERN SHORTFIN SQUID *Ilex illecebrosus*

PELAGIC CRUSTACEANS
__ EDIBLE PENAEUS SHRIMP *Penaeus* spp.
__ NORTHERN SHRIMP (Boreal Red Shrimp) *Pandalus* spp.
__ SLENDER SARGASSUM SHRIMP (Gulfweed Shrimp) *Latreutes fucorum*

SPECIES CHECKLIST
SHARKS AND RAYS

SHARKS
__ BLACKTIP SHARK *Carcharhinus limbatus*
__ BLUE SHARK *Prionace glauca*
__ BULL SHARK *Carcharhinus leucas*
__ DUSKY SHARK *Carcharhinus obscurus*
__ LONGFIN MAKO *Isurus paucus*
__ NURSE SHARK *Ginglymostoma cirratum*
__ OCEANIC WHITETIP SHARK *Carcharhinus longimanus*
__ PORBEAGLE *Lamna nasus*
__ SANDBAR SHARK (Brown Shark) *Carcharhinus plumbeus*
__ SAND TIGER (Sand Shark) *Carcharias taurus*
__ SHORTFIN MAKO *Isurus oxyrhinchus*
__ SILKY ("SICKLE") SHARK *Carcharhinus falciformis*
__ SPINNER SHARK *Carcharhinus brevipinna*
__ TIGER SHARK *Galeocerdo cuvier*
__ WHITE SHARK *Carcharodon carcharias*

THRESHER SHARKS
__ BIGEYE THRESHER *Alopias superciliosus*
__ THRESHER SHARK *Alopias vulpinus*

HAMMERHEAD SHARKS
__ BONNETHEAD SHARK *Sphyrna tiburo*
__ GREAT HAMMERHEAD *Sphyrna mokarran*
__ GREENLAND SHARK *Somniosus microcephalus*
__ PORTUGUESE SHARK *Centroscymnus coelolepis*
__ SCALLOPED HAMMERHEAD *Sphyrna lewini*
__ SIXGILL SHARK *Hexanchus griseus*
__ SMOOTH HAMMERHEAD *Sphyrna zygaena*

DOGFISH
__ BLACK DOGFISH *Centroscyllium fabricii*
__ SMOOTH DOGFISH *Mustelus canis*
__ SPINY DOGFISH *Squalus acanthias*

GIANT SHARKS
__ BASKING SHARK *Cetorhinus maximus*
__ WHALE SHARK *Rhincodon typus*

PELAGIC RAYS
__ ATLANTIC MANTA (Devilfish) *Manta birostris*
__ DEVIL RAY *Mobula hypostoma*
__ SPOTTED EAGLE RAY *Myliobatis aquila*

FISH

PILOTFISH, REMORAS
__ PILOTFISH *Naucrates ductor*
__ REMORA *Remora remora*
__ SHARKSUCKER *Echeneis naucrates*
__ WHITEFIN SHARKSUCKER *Echeneis neucratoides*

PUFFERS, PORCUPINEFISH
__ NORTHERN PUFFER *Sphoeroides maculatus*
__ OCEANIC PUFFER *Lagocephalus lagocephalus*
__ PORCUPINEFISH *Diodon hystrix*
__ SMOOTH PUFFER *Lagocephalus laevigatus*
__ SPOTTED BURRFISH *Chilomycterus atringa*

HERRING, SHAD, MENHADEN
__ ALEWIFE *Alosa pseudoharengus*
__ AMERICAN SHAD *Alosa sapidissima*
__ ATLANTIC HERRING *Clupea harengus*
__ ATLANTIC MENHADEN (Mossbunker) *Brevoortia tyrannus*
__ BLUEBACK HERRING *Alosa aestivalis*
__ HICKORY SHAD *Alosa mediocris*

CODS
__ ATLANTIC COD *Gadus morhua*
__ CUSK *Brosme brosme*
__ HADDOCK *Melanogrammus aeglefinus*
__ POLLOCK *Pollachius virens*
__ SILVER HAKE *Merluccius bilinearis*
__ WHITE HAKE *Urophycis tenuis*

FLYINGFISH
__ ATLANTIC FLYINGFISH *Cheilopogon melanurus*
__ BANDWING FLYINGFISH *Cheilopogon exsiliens*
__ MARGINED FLYINGFISH *Cypselurus cyanopterus*
__ OCEANIC TWO-WING FLYINGFISH *Exocoetus obtusirostris*
__ SPOTFIN FLYINGFISH *Cheilopogon furcatus*

SPECIES CHECKLIST

POMPANOS, JACKS
__ AFRICAN POMPANO *Alectis ciliaris*
__ CREVALLE JACK *Caranx hippos*
__ FLORIDA POMPANO *Trachinotus carolinus*
__ HORSE-EYE JACK *Caranx latus*
__ PERMIT *Trachinotus falcatus*
__ YELLOW JACK *Carangoides bartholomaei*

DOLPHINS, LOUVAR, OPAH
__ DOLPHIN (Dorado) *Coryphaena hippurus*
__ LOUVAR *Luvarus imperialis*
__ OPAH *Lampris guttatus*
__ POMPANO DOLPHIN *Coryphaena equiselis*

GAME FISH
__ ACADIAN REDFISH *Sebastes fasciatus*
__ ATLANTIC SALMON *Salmo salar*
__ BLACK SEA BASS *Centropristis striata*
__ BLUEFISH *Pomatomus saltatrix*
__ COBIA *Rachycentron canadum*
__ CUNNER *Tautogolabrus adspersus*
__ GREAT BARRACUDA *Sphyraena borealis*
__ SCUP (Porgy) *Stenotomus chrysops*
__ STRIPED BASS *Morone saxatilis*
__ TAUTOG *Tautoga onitis*
__ WEAKFISH *Cynoscion regalis*
__ WHITE PERCH *Morone americana*

BALLYHOO, NEEDLEFISH, SAND LANCE
__ ATLANTIC NEEDLEFISH *Strongylura marina*
__ BALAO *Hemiramphus balao*
__ BALLYHOO *Hemiramphus brasiliensis*
__ HALFBEAK *Hyporhamphus unifasciatus*
__ NORTHERN SAND LANCE *Ammodytes dubius*

MACKEREL
__ ATLANTIC MACKEREL *Scomber scombrus*
__ CERO *Scomberomorus regalis*
__ KING MACKEREL *Scomberomorus cavalla*
__ SPANISH MACKEREL *Scomberomorus maculatus*
__ WAHOO *Acanthocybium solandri*

TUNA
__ ALBACORE *Thunnus alalunga*
__ ATLANTIC BONITO *Sarda sarda*
__ BIGEYE TUNA *Thunnus obesus*
__ BLACKFIN TUNA *Thunnus atlanticus*
__ BLUEFIN TUNA *Thunnus thynnus*
__ BULLET MACKEREL *Auxis rochei*
__ FRIGATE MACKEREL *Auxis thazard*
__ LITTLE TUNNY *Euthynnus alletteratus*
__ SKIPJACK TUNA *Euthynnus pelamis*
__ YELLOWFIN TUNA *Thunnus albacares*

BILLFISH
__ BLUE MARLIN *Makaira nigricans*
__ LONGBILL SPEARFISH *Tetrapturus pfluegeri*
__ SAILFISH *Istiophorus platypterus*
__ SWORDFISH *Xiphias gladius*
__ WHITE MARLIN *Tetrapturus albidus*

SCULPINS AND SEAROBIN
__ LONGHORN SCULPIN *Myoxocephalus octodecemspinosus*
__ NORTHERN SEAROBIN *Prionotus carolinus*
__ SEA RAVEN *Hemitripterus americanus*
__ SHORTHORN SCULPIN *Myoxocephalus scorpius*

FLOUNDERS, HALIBUT, GOOSEFISH
__ ATLANTIC HALIBUT *Hippoglossus hippoglossus*
__ GOOSEFISH *Lophius americanus*
__ SUMMER FLOUNDER *Paralichthys dentatus*
__ WINTER FLOUNDER (Lemon Sole) *Pseudopleuronectes americanus*

OCEAN SUNFISH
__ OCEAN SUNFISH *Mola mola*
__ SHARPTAIL MOLA *Masturus lanceolatus*

REPTILES

SEA TURTLES
__ ATLANTIC HAWKSBILL *Eretmochelys imbricata*
__ ATLANTIC LEATHERBACK *Dermochelys coriacea*
__ ATLANTIC RIDLEY *Lepidochelys kempi*
__ GREEN SEA TURTLE *Chelonia mydas*
__ LOGGERHEAD SEA TURTLE *Caretta caretta*

207

SPECIES CHECKLIST

BIRDS

LOONS AND GREBES
__ COMMON LOON *Gavia immer*
__ HORNED GREBE *Podiceps auritus*
__ RED-NECKED GREBE *Podiceps grisegena*
__ RED-THROATED LOON *Gavia stellata*

ALBATROSSES, TROPICBIRD, FRIGATEBIRD
__ BLACK-BROWED ALBATROSS *Diomedea melanophris*
__ MAGNIFICENT FRIGATEBIRD *Fregata magnificens*
__ WHITE-TAILED TROPICBIRD *Phaethon lepturus*
__ YELLOW-NOSED ALBATROSS *Diomedea chlororhynchos*

SHEARWATERS AND PETRELS
__ AUDUBON'S SHEARWATER *Puffinus lherminieri*
__ BLACK-CAPPED PETREL *Pterodroma hasitata*
__ CORY'S SHEARWATER *Calonectris diomedea*
__ GREATER SHEARWATER *Puffinus gravis*
__ HERALD (TRINIDAD) PETREL *Pterodroma arminjoniana*
__ LITTLE SHEARWATER *Puffinus assimilis*
__ MANX SHEARWATER *Puffinus puffinus*
__ NORTHERN FULMAR *Fulmarus glacialis*
__ SOFT-PLUMAGED (FEA'S) PETREL *Pterodroma feae*
__ SOOTY SHEARWATER *Puffinus griseus*

STORM-PETRELS
__ BAND-RUMPED STORM-PETREL *Oceanodroma castro*
__ LEACH'S STORM-PETREL *Oceanodroma leucorhoa*
__ WHITE-FACED STORM-PETREL *Pelagodroma marina*
__ WILSON'S STORM-PETREL *Oceanites oceanicus*

PELICAN
__ BROWN PELICAN *Pelecanus occidentalis*

GANNET AND BOOBIES
__ BROWN BOOBY *Sula dactylatra*
__ MASKED BOOBY *Sula leucogaster*
__ NORTHERN GANNET *Morus bassanus*

CORMORANTS
__ DOUBLE-CRESTED CORMORANT *Phalacrocorax auritus*
__ GREAT CORMORANT *Phalacrocorax carbo*

OSPREY AND NIGHT-HERON
__ BLACK-CROWNED NIGHT-HERON *Nycticorax nycticorax*
__ OSPREY *Pandion haliaetus*

BRANT AND DUCKS
__ BARROW'S GOLDENEYE *Bucephala islandica*
__ BLACK SCOTER *Melanitta nigra*
__ BRANT *Branta bernicla*
__ BUFFLEHEAD *Bucephala albeola*
__ COMMON EIDER *Somateria mollissima*
__ COMMON GOLDENEYE *Bucephala clangula*
__ GREATER SCAUP *Aythya marila*
__ HARLEQUIN DUCK *Histrionicus histrionicus*
__ KING EIDER *Somateria spectabilis*
__ LESSER SCAUP *Aythya affinis*
__ LONG-TAILED DUCK *Clangula hyemalis*
__ RED-BREASTED MERGANSER *Mergus serrator*
__ SURF SCOTER *Melanitta perspicillata*
__ WHITE-WINGED SCOTER *Melanitta fusca*

SHOREBIRDS
__ AMERICAN GOLDEN-PLOVER *Pluvialis dominica*
__ RED-NECKED PHALAROPE *Phalaropus lobatus*
__ RED PHALAROPE *Phalaropus fulicaria*
__ WHIMBREL *Numenius phaeopus*

SKUAS AND JAEGERS
__ GREAT SKUA *Catharacta skua*
__ LONG-TAILED JAEGER *Stercorarius longicaudus*
__ PARASITIC JAEGER *Stercorarius parasiticus*
__ POMARINE JAEGER *Stercorarius pomarinus*
__ SOUTH POLAR SKUA *Catharacta maccormicki*

GULLS
__ BLACK-HEADED GULL *Larus ridibundus*
__ BLACK-LEGGED KITTIWAKE *Rissa tridactyla*
__ BONAPARTE'S GULL *Larus philadelphia*
__ GLAUCOUS GULL *Larus hyperboreus*
__ GREAT BLACK-BACKED GULL *Larus marinus*
__ HERRING GULL *Larus argentatus*
__ ICELAND GULL *Larus glaucoides*
__ IVORY GULL *Pagophila eburnea*
__ LAUGHING GULL *Larus atricilla*

SPECIES CHECKLIST

GULLS *(continued)*
__ LESSER BLACK-BACKED GULL *Larus fuscus*
__ LITTLE GULL *Larus minutus*
__ RING-BILLED GULL *Larus delawarensis*
__ ROSS'S GULL *Rhodostethia rosea*
__ SABINE'S GULL *Xema sabini*

TERNS
__ ARCTIC TERN *Sterna paradisaea*
__ BLACK NODDY *Anous minutus*
__ BLACK SKIMMER *Rhynchops niger*
__ BLACK TERN *Chlidonias niger*
__ BRIDLED TERN *Sterna anaethetus*
__ BROWN NODDY *Anous stolidus*
__ CASPIAN TERN *Sterna caspia*
__ COMMON TERN *Sterna hirundo*
__ FORSTER'S TERN *Sterna forsteri*
__ GULL-BILLED TERN *Sterna nilotica*
__ LEAST TERN *Sterna antillarum*
__ ROSEATE TERN *Sterna dougallii*
__ ROYAL TERN *Sterna maxima*
__ SANDWICH TERN *Sterna sandvicensis*
__ SOOTY TERN *Sterna fuscata*

ALCIDS
__ ATLANTIC PUFFIN *Fratercula arctica*
__ BLACK GUILLEMOT *Cepphus grylle*
__ COMMON MURRE *Uria aalge*
__ DOVEKIE *Alle alle*
__ RAZORBILL *Alca torda*
__ THICK-BILLED MURRE *Uria lomvia*

WHALES AND DOLPHINS

RORQUALS
__ BLUE WHALE *Balaenoptera musculus*
__ BRYDE'S WHALE *Balaenoptera brydei*
__ FIN WHALE *Balaenoptera physalus*
__ HUMPBACK WHALE *Megaptera novaeangliae*
__ MINKE WHALE *Balaenoptera acutorostrata*
__ SEI WHALE *Balaenoptera borealis*

RIGHT WHALE
__ NORTHERN RIGHT WHALE *Eubalaena glacialis*

TOOTHED WHALES
__ BELUGA *Delphinapterus leucas*
__ BLAINVILLE'S BEAKED WHALE *Mesoplodon densirostris*
__ CUVIER'S BEAKED WHALE *Ziphius cavirostris*
__ DWARF SPERM WHALE *Kogia simus*
__ FALSE KILLER WHALE *Pseudorca crassidens*
__ GRAMPUS *Grampus griseus*
__ KILLER WHALE (ORCA) *Orcinus orca*
__ LONG-FINNED PILOT WHALE *Globicephala melas*
__ NORTHERN BOTTLENOSE WHALE *Hyperoodon ampullatus*
__ PYGMY SPERM WHALE *Kogia breviceps*
__ SHORT-FINNED PILOT WHALE *Globicephala macrorhynchus*
__ SOWERBY'S BEAKED WHALE *Mesoplodon bidens*
__ SPERM WHALE *Physeter macrocephalus*
__ TRUE'S BEAKED WHALE *Mesoplodon mirus*

DOLPHINS AND PORPOISE
__ ATLANTIC SPOTTED DOLPHIN *Stenella frontalis*
__ ATLANTIC WHITE-SIDED DOLPHIN *Lagenorhynchus acutus*
__ BOTTLENOSE DOLPHIN *Tursiops truncatus*
__ CLYMENE DOLPHIN *Stenella clymene*
__ COMMON DOLPHIN *Delphinus delphis*
__ HARBOR PORPOISE *Phocoena phocoena*
__ LONG-SNOUTED SPINNER DOLPHIN *Stenella longirostris*
__ PANTROPICAL SPOTTED DOLPHIN *Stenella attenuata*
__ ROUGH-TOOTHED DOLPHIN *Steno bredanensis*
__ SPINNER DOLPHIN *Stenella longirostris*
__ STRIPED DOLPHIN *Stenella coeruleoalba*
__ WHITE-BEAKED DOLPHIN *Lagenorhynchus albirostris*

SEALS

__ GRAY SEAL *Halichoerus grypus*
__ HARBOR SEAL *Phoca vitulina*
__ HARP SEAL *Pagophilus groenlandicus*
__ HOODED SEAL *Cystophora cristata*
__ RINGED SEAL *Phoca hispida*

GLOSSARY

abyssal plain – The vast, relatively flat ocean floor, at a general depth of 9,500–16,500 ft. (3,000–5,000 m).

anadromous – Fish such as salmon or shad that spend most of their lives at sea but return to freshwater rivers to breed.

bank – A shallow area on the continental shelf. Banks are usually rich in prey fish, predatory fish, marine mammals, and seabirds.

baleen – Comb-like rows of flexible plates that project downward from the upper jaws of some whales and aid in filter-feeding for plankton. The baleen plates act as a giant sieve, helping the whale to extract plankton from seawater.

benthic – Pertaining to the ocean floor or to the environment and organisms of the ocean floor.

benthos – Marine organisms that live on or near the ocean floor.

blooms – Dense concentrations of phytoplankton, generally in areas unusually rich in nutrients and with optimal growth conditions.

blow – The first – and very large – exhalation of breath a whale makes when surfacing from a dive. Typically a powerful jet of extremely humid air that immediately condenses into a visible "spout" above the whale's nostrils. Its shape is a useful long-distance field mark for identifying whales. In large whales the blow may be heard for long distances.

breach – A leap out of or nearly free of the water by a whale, dolphin, or fish. A social common behavior in Humpback Whales. Some species of large game fish like tuna and marlin jump free of the surface while actively chasing prey.

bubble cloud – A Humpback Whale will often dive below a school of small prey fish and release a massive "cloud" of bubbles to force the school up against the surface, where the whale can more easily attack them. As the cloud rises, watch for the feeding whale to lunge up through the middle of the bubble cloud, usually breaking the surface with its mouth wide open and then sliding back down to let the water and fish pour in as it submerges.

bubble netting – A feeding Humpback Whale will sometimes swim around the periphery of a school of prey fish while exhaling a steady stream of bubbles to form a "net" around the school. The frightened fish are reluctant to cross through the bubble net, making it easier for the whale to lunge into the school and swallow its prey.

GLOSSARY

catadromous – Fish that spend most of their lives in fresh water but migrate to salt water to breed. American and European eels are catadromous.

caudal – Toward the tail or relating to the tail.

caudal fin – The large fin at the posterior end of most fish species; commonly called the tail fin.

cephalic – Toward the head, or relating to the head.

cetacean – An animal of the taxonomic order Cetacea, which comprises whales, dolphins, and porpoises.

continental shelf – The usually flat and relatively shallow sea floor that extends out from the shoreline to a depth of about 650 ft. (200 m).

continental slope – The (usually) steep underwater slope that drops from the relatively shallow continental shelf waters to the deep ocean bed, or abyssal plain.

diadromous – Fish that migrate between fresh water and salt water. Includes both anadromous and catadromous fish.

dorsal – The upper, back, or spinal side of an organism.

dorsal fin – A single vertical fin that projects upward from the top ridge of the back. Most sharks and many bony fish have two dorsal fins. Whales and dolphins that have a dorsal fin (not all do) have a single fin.

epifauna – Animals that live on a surface; the ocean bottom surface, or in the surface and uppermost layers of the water.

epipelagic – Upper area of the open ocean waters, down to a depth of 300 ft. (100 m).

estuary – An ecological area of mixed salt and fresh water, where a river meets the sea.

fetch – The distance over open water that winds blow to create waves. In general, the longer the fetch, the larger the waves that are blown up.

flukes – The paired flat, horizontal halves of a whale's tail.

footprint – Large, smooth patch of surface water formed by the powerful upward tail strokes of an actively swimming whale. A whale cruising just below the surface will often leave a series of huge "footprints" across the water's surface.

invertebrates – Animals without backbones, such as jellyfish, shrimp, and squid.

krill – Tiny, shrimp-like crustaceans often found in dense masses in the open ocean or in especially nutrient-rich waters.

ledge – A small bank or relatively shallow area that rises sharply from the continental shelf and is attractive to fish, marine mammals, and seabirds. Examples: Coxes Ledge off Montauk Point and Jeffreys Ledge off New Hampshire in the Gulf of Maine.

littoral – The intertidal zone, immediately adjacent to the shore.

nekton – Active, swimming marine animals larger than a few inches in length. Includes sharks, fish, marine reptiles, and marine mammals.

oceanic – Pertaining to the deepest waters above the deep ocean basins, far offshore.

operculum – The bony hinged plate that covers and protects the gills and gill arches of bony fish.

pectoral fin – One of a pair of fins anatomically associated with the chest, corresponding to arms in humans. In bony fish the pectoral fins are located immediately behind the gills, along the sides of the body. In sharks the pectoral fins emerge low on the body behind the gill slits. In skates and rays the "wings" are modified pectoral fins.

pelagic – Pertaining to the deep-water marine environment well away from the coast and the animals that inhabit the deep ocean.

pelvic fin – One of a pair of fins associated with the pelvic bones, corresponding to legs in humans. In most bony fish the pelvic fins are located along the bottom edge of the body, just behind the pectoral fins. In sharks the pelvic fins are well to the rear of the pectoral fins.

phytoplankton – Microscopic algae and other microorganisms that photosynthesize, as in green plants.

pod – A group of whales. Most often used to describe semi-permanent social groups of medium-sized toothed whales or dolphins.

GLOSSARY

red tide – A major bloom of red-colored planktonic dinoflagellates (tiny marine organisms) that produce toxins that often kill many other marine animals that enter the "red tide" area.

rorquals – A group of whale species in the family Balaenopteridae (Blue, Fin, Sei, Bryde's, Minke, Humpback) with deep longitudinal grooves along the length of the throat that permit its vast expansion when feeding.

Sargasso Sea – An area of the central Atlantic Ocean just north of the Equator characterized by a circular current that tends to isolate those waters from the surrounding Atlantic currents. The Sargasso Sea is warm and relatively calm, and large mats of marine algae, called Gulfweed or Sargassum Weed, cover much of its surface.

spy-hop – Humpback Whales, seals, some dolphins, and even such sharks as the White Shark will poke their heads above the surface to look around, a behavior known as "spy-hopping."

tail roll – The slow, rolling emergence of the tail flukes in a whale that is beginning a deep dive. A common behavior of Humpback and Sperm Whales; much less common in shallow-diving rorquals like the Fin and Sei Whales.

temperature gradient shock – Sudden changes in water temperature can kill or shock fish into a stupor, such as when warm-water species coming north on the Gulf Stream are suddenly exposed to cold northern waters.

trade winds – Subtropical winds that blow from the northeast to the southwest in the Northern Hemisphere.

tube-noses – Shearwaters, petrels, and albatrosses. Refers to the tube-like nostrils on the bills of these seabird families, that are specialized to help the birds exude excess salts from drinking seawater.

upwelling – A vertical, upward movement of water that typically carries nutrients from deeper waters toward the surface. Areas of upwelling are rich in marine life.

ventral – The lower or belly side of an organism.

zooplankton – Animal members of the plankton, which typically do not use photosynthesis, as in the phytoplankton.

INDEX

INDEX

INDEX

220

FIELD NOTES

FIELD NOTES

FIELD NOTES

FIELD NOTES

FIELD NOTES

FIELD NOTES